TWO
MIGHTY
RIVERS

CAN THE SON OF AN INDIAN PRINCESS AND
AN ENGLISH PIONEER BUILD A BRIDGE BETWEEN
TWO WORLDS AT WAR?

• • •

TWO
MIGHTY
RIVERS

———

Son of Pocahontas

• • •

MARI HANES

GOLD 'N' HONEY BOOKS
SISTERS, OREGON

TWO MIGHTY RIVERS

published by Multnomah Books
a part of the Questar publishing family

© 1995 by Mari Dunagan Hanes
Illustrations © 1996 by David Danz

International Standard Book Number: 0-88070-999-5

Cover illustration by Paul Bachem
Cover design by David Carlson

Printed in the United States of America

Most scripture quotations are from the *New International Version* © 1973, 1984 by
International Bible Society used by permission of Zondervan Publishing House.

Also quoted:
The *New American Standard Bible* © 1969, 1977 by
the Lockman Foundation; used by permission.
The *International Children's Bible, New Century Version* © 1986, 1988 by
Word Publishing; used by permission.
The Living Bible © 1971 by Tyndal House Publishers.
The *King James Version* (KJV)

For information:
Questar Publishers, Inc.
Post Office Box 1720
Sisters, Oregon 97759

96 97 98 99 00 01 02 03 — 10 9 8 7 6 5 4 3 2 1

In memory of my father,

James Dunagan,

who died when I was young,

but whose wisdom and goodness will always be with me.

CONTENTS

INTRODUCTION

Four hundred years ago, a young Algonquin girl lived her life with such faith and courage she is still remembered today. You can read her true story in the book *Pocahontas: True Princess*.

Pocahontas married a handsome Englishman named John Rolfe. She and John had a baby boy whom they named Thomas. Pocahontas' father, the great chief Powhatan, gave him another name: Pepsicanough.

This book is the amazing story of Thomas Pepsicanough Rolfe. His exciting adventures transport the reader to another time and place. Caught between two warring cultures, Thomas is encouraged by his dear English friend, Jane Poythress, and his Algonquin uncle, Parahunt. His greatest challenge is to discover which of these two worlds he belongs in—and it is a long, hard, journey that only he can travel. Yet along the way, he finds that God has a perfect plan for his life which gives him the best of both worlds.

CHAPTER ONE

STRANGE RIDER

THOMAS BENT LOW in his saddle and urged his horse up the rocky hill. The wind blew fiercely across the moor, but he didn't mind. He loved Scotland's wild weather and rugged countryside. This was the way he imagined his true homeland would look—far across the sea.

When he reached the top of the hill he slid smoothly from his saddle to the ground and patted the neck of his powerful horse. "Good job, Moco," he said. He dropped the reins and the tall black thoroughbred began to graze on the rich highland grass.

The hem of his cloak snapped in the wind as he pressed toward the edge of the rocky hilltop. He narrowed his eyes against the sharp sea breeze and sighed deeply. There beyond the moor lay the gray choppy ocean, the mighty Atlantic, and beyond that was the Chesapeake.

Thomas peered longingly toward that unseen world, that wild and beautiful land of the mighty Algonquin people, the homeland of his mother, the beautiful Princess Pocahontas. Thomas had been born there. And now his father, John Rolfe, stayed in a place called Jamestown.

"I am missing you, Father!" Thomas shouted, but his words were snatched away by the wind. If only they could be swept across the wide grey sea. Thomas wasn't sorry that he had slipped away from the hunting party of friends and relatives. They were busy scouting deer and pheasant on the royal game reserve; they probably wouldn't miss him. Besides, he needed to be alone.

A familiar screeching cry drew his eyes upward. The sight of his grandfather's hunting falcon always thrilled him. He knew the powerful bird would dive down to perch on his arm if he raised a gloved hand as a signal. But he did not. "Fly free, Lightning," he whispered. "I have no reason to call you back to earth. And if I had *your* wings, I'd fly far from here and join my father."

He dropped to the ground and sat with his legs crossed. Huddled against the wind, he pulled a treasure from a pocket of his woolen cloak. He carefully smoothed the yellowed parchment and traced each letter his father had penned.

> *My beloved son Thomas,*
>
> *Since I last wrote to you, I have received the honor of being named one of the new Governors of Jamestown. My duties at the fort are many...*
>
> *Still, I am most happy when I am able to spend time at the church school with Reverend Thorpe. We have both Indian and English students at the school now. I know that would mean so much to your mother, for this was her dream.*
>
> *I have labored long and hard this harvest season on our land here. But I have not changed anything in the home that I built, the house called Varina that your mother loved so much.*
>
> *I often sit in the little bedroom where you*

were born; the room where Pocahontas sang you
to sleep, the room where we laughed at the funny
way you took your first steps.

The English cradle I built for you is still here.
Your mother always insisted on lacing you into an
Algonquin cradle-board before she would lay you
in it, and the memory of her ways delights me!

Your little hands would reach up to play
with the tiny sea shells that she had sewn to hang
down in rows from the roof of the cradle-board.
They were your first toys...

He did not need to read the rest of the letter. Every word
was stored securely in his memory. He hugged the paper tightly
against his chest. In his mind Father's words continued:

This past summer I received the sad news of
the death of your grandfather, Powhatan, the
great chief of many tribes and the father of your
own dear mother. He had come to love the ways
of peace, and in his last days had gone to live
among the Potomac tribe.

How I wish you had seen that mighty old
man standing tall as a giant! And now I've
received letters saying that you have inherited
Powhatan's strength and stature.

I pray for you daily, my dear Son. I am
strengthened by the thought that you shall soon
join me.

Your Loving Father,
John Rolfe

Thomas refolded the letter and returned it to the deep pocket of his cloak. He brushed the back of his hand impatiently across his eyes and swallowed hard. The grandson of a mighty Algonquin chief would not cry.

The thunder of hoof beats jolted his attention back to the moor. In the meadow below raced a horse as powerful as Moco. On this horse's back clung a rider who seemed to have lost all control of his mount!

The horse leaped over hedges and rock fences as its clinging passenger bounced in the saddle. They were headed right in the direction of the large hunting party! Even if this young rider survived the wild ride, he might be caught in the crossfire of the powerful hunting guns.

Thomas sprang onto Moco's back and urged him down the hill. "Faster, boy!" He felt the blood rush to his head. If he didn't reach him in time, that boy's runaway ride might be his last!

The other horse was surprisingly fast, but Thomas knew he was no match to his own powerful horse. He quickly reined Moco directly alongside the rider's path. Now Thomas drew close enough to see the rider was only a child, even younger than himself. Moco sailed like a racehorse over the roughness of the moor, and soon pulled even with the other horse. Just as they reached the edge of the meadow, Thomas strained forward. He balanced against Moco's powerful neck, and reached out to grab the runaway's reins. As soon as he had a firm grasp he reined back Moco and jerked the other horse to a halt.

The sudden stop threw the other rider off balance. A terrified scream split the air as the surprised rider flew from the horse and thudded to the ground. Thomas leaped off Moco and dropped to his hands and knees beside the small, motionless body. The stranger's face was pale and the eyes were closed.

"Please, be all right!" Thomas commanded, gasping for air. "I had to keep you from the path of the hunters!" At last, the child's mouth opened as he struggled to catch his breath. Thomas reached down and tugged at the chin straps of his riding hat, allowing the helmet to slip from the fallen rider's head. Thomas blinked in surprise as a river of reddish-brown curls tumbled loose from the hat. He jerked back in shock as long lashes fluttered open to reveal big blue eyes. The rider was a girl! And after that hard fall, she was actually grinning!

"What a foolish thing to do!" he yelled. "What a dangerous thing to do! A girl has no business racing a horse across these rough moors! You were headed straight toward our hunting party. You could have been killed!" He stood, and backed away sputtering.

She pushed herself up and brushed off her riding breeches, then slowly rose to her feet. Thomas was too upset to lend her a hand. Even when she stood up straight, the top of her head barely reached his shoulder.

She took in a deep breath and smiled, holding out her hand in greeting. But Thomas backed away, still muttering. "A girl! On a horse such as that!"

To his amazement she laughed out loud. "Why should *you* be surprised that a girl can have courage?" she asked. "Aren't *you* the son of the courageous *Pocahontas?*"

"Yes, I am." He stood straighter, taller. "I am Thomas Pepsicanough Rolfe."

"And I've come here looking for you," she announced. "And, I've decided to call you Pepsi."

"No one calls me that!"

"Well, I shall. Thomas is much too common a name for you, to my way of thinking."

"And who might *you* be?" he scowled.

"I'm Janie Poythress, and my father is Colonel Poythress who works for the Virginia Company. We've come all the way to Scotland just to see you and your grandfather. My father stayed back at the hunting lodge, but I rode out to find you." She held her chin out and continued. "I'm very happy we can finally meet. I've heard stories about Jamestown and the brave Princess Pocahontas all my life."

Once again, Janie extended her hand to Thomas, but he turned away. He watched from the corner of his eye as she stiffly walked to where her horse grazed nearby. It seemed the rough ride and even rougher landing had not harmed her.

"I'm planning to return to Jamestown," he offered, but even as the words escaped his lips he wondered why he should share this important information with a foolish girl.

"That's a long voyage. Are you afraid of crossing the sea?"

"No, of course not! Haven't I already done it once?"

"But that was long ago, and you were so young."

"Oh, I remember a lot about it," he assured her. Still, he wasn't positive the memories were really his. Maybe he only *thought* he remembered, because his family so often talked about his past.

"What do you remember?"

"I remember the very day we left Jamestown. I was carried up the gangplank on my father's shoulders. My mother's sister and several great Algonquin warriors followed us onto the ship. A princess like my mother would never travel to visit a foreign ruler like King James without attendants."

Janie nodded, her eyes wide with admiration.

"When we sailed out into the river," he continued, "a great Algonquin war canoe came alongside the English ship. The warriors wore bright feathers and red paint. In the middle stood my grandfather, Powhatan. Mother held me up and said, 'Wave, young Thomas. Wave goodbye to your grandfather.' When tears rolled down my face, she said, 'Don't cry, Son. Algonquins do not behave this way. Someday you will return to this land!'"

Thomas paused, lost in thought, until Janie asked, "And what do you remember of the ocean voyage?"

"I remember the fun of trying to walk on the deck as the ship rolled and tossed on the Great Sea. I remember my mother's proud laughter as she held out her hands to me. I remember the sound of her singing. She sang story-songs of my people, and lullabies, and hymns of praise to God."

His words slowed again. Was he saying too much to this strange girl? Yet something about her made it easy to talk.

"And when you docked in England," Janie said, "there was a cheering crowd to meet you. Right?"

Thomas turned and stared into her sparkling blue eyes. "How did you know that?"

"The captain told me. He said your mother was already famous in England."

"The captain?"

"Yes, Captain John Smith. He's the one who brought my father here to meet you. He talked about Pocahontas all the way here from London to here. You do remember him, don't you?"

Captain John Smith! The great man of Jamestown—the friend of his mother! And he was here! In one smooth movement Thomas turned and jumped astride his mount.

"Follow me!" he commanded Janie over his shoulder. He reined Moco's head toward the hunting lodge and urged the horse into a run.

Thomas' heart pounded with excitement as he rode. If Captain John Smith had come to visit, maybe the Company had decided to send him back to Jamestown! And if that was true, maybe the captain would take Thomas with him!

CHAPTER TWO

CAPTAIN JOHN SMITH

MOCO EASILY FOLLOWED the well-known path back to the hunting lodge. Thomas glanced over his shoulder to make sure Janie's horse was following as they cut through the field of heather. High overhead, grandfather's hunting falcon still circled. The great bird slowly soared around, just like the many thoughts that whirled through Thomas' mind. Janie's persistent questions about his first voyage had triggered many childhood memories.

He remembered the noise and the crowds of the jumbled brick city called London. He had never seen so many people in one place! He remembered the bumpity feeling of his first carriage ride, and even the taste of strange sweets placed in his mouth by friendly people who wore lots of funny clothes.

He could still see the innkeeper's puzzled face when Father arranged for great tubs of water to be brought up, so that Mother and the other Algonquins could enjoy their daily bath.

And he would never forget their visit to the Royal Court. All around him, Thomas had heard people say, 'Pocahontas is so lovely! Such a true princess!' Even this childhood memory could stir the same feeling of pride, to know they had been talking about *his* mother.

He also remembered how clumsy he felt when Mother prompted him to perform a bow when he was presented to Queen Anne. But the round-faced Queen just smiled and ruffled his hair, and he had liked her very much.

But mostly he remembered Mother. So beautiful, so full of joy. No one was ever so gentle and kind. And he had never heard a harsh word cross between Mother and Father. They had been very happy. But how quickly things had changed....

A brisk wind arose and whipped up his cloak. He hunched down and continued to ride. He didn't want to face the next memory that had crept into his thoughts. But it was too late; the picture in his mind was too sharp, too clear. He knew it would not leave unless he allowed himself to look, to remember....

It was supposed to have been a joyous trip. They were returning back to the Chesapeake. But shortly after the voyage began, Mother was struck down with a fever. He still remembered how hot she felt when his small hand touched her forehead, and the frightened look in her eyes as she looked up at him. But this awful memory was always blurred by pain and confusion, for soon after, he too was swallowed up by the sickness. After that he recalled being rocked in the arms of Grandmother and Grandfather Rolfe. He remembered crying quietly when he learned that Mother was gone, and Father was so very far away....

Thomas slowly shook his head as Moco turned down the long lane of the hunting lodge. Janie still followed quietly behind him. He was thankful she wasn't a girl who liked to jabber. He must shake these gloomy memories from his mind. After all, today was a day to rejoice! He would see the great Captain John Smith today!

He hadn't seen the captain since right after Mother was buried in the town of Gravesend. Thomas recalled sitting upon Captain Smith's knee, and listening to the captain tell of his mother, the Princess Pocahontas.

"When your mother was a young girl, she saved my life, and the lives of many in Jamestown. She was as dear to me as if she were my daughter...." And then great tears rolled from the captain's ocean-blue eyes. Thomas remembered watching them slide down his cheeks and into his flowing, golden-red beard.

But now the captain was here—and it would be such fun to see him! Perhaps the captain would return to Jamestown. Maybe Thomas could go with him! If only Captain Smith could convince Grandfather that Thomas didn't need to finish his schooling. Maybe he could even make Grandfather understand that Thomas should be with his father.

Just when he reached the gate of the hunting lodge, Janie galloped up to his side. She rode fairly well for a girl, and she hadn't complained once about the fall. He turned in her direction with a smile. He didn't quite know how to apologize for his earlier rudeness, but he hoped she might understand.

A groomsman met them and led away the horses. "I will brush your mounts well for ye. Ye have certainly worked Moco into quite a lather!"

"Moco..." Jane repeated. "That's an unusual name for a horse."

"It comes from the word Werowocomoco, the name of my

mother's Algonquin village," Thomas explained. "But I could never say that when I was little. So I just named him Moco."

"Watch as I call in our falcon," Thomas said, as he slipped on a heavy leather glove, and extended his arm. High overhead, the falcon waited for this movement from his young master. Thomas knew the bird's keen eyes had observed the signal as the falcon appeared to fall straight down from the sky like a cannon ball. Janie ducked behind Thomas as the huge falcon broke its fall with a great flutter of wings, then landed on Thomas' arm with smooth perfection.

"That was amazing!" she exclaimed. Thomas silently basked in her admiration as he placed the small leather hood over the bird's eyes. Janie followed as Thomas carried the falcon to a special perch in a corner building of the stable yard.

"This wooden roost is called a cadge," he explained to Jane as he put Lightning in her place beside the other hooded birds. Thomas pointed to an enormous golden eagle also on the cadge. "This great hunter is called Majesty. And that smaller bird is a Merlin hawk. It goes out hunting with ladies." He could see that Janie was impressed, and her blue eyes glowed with interest. His girl cousins had no interest in hunting birds, but he was starting to think that Janie was not an ordinary girl.

Suddenly he remembered the special visitor who was waiting. "Come on, Janie! Let's go find the captain!" he urged.

He ran through the front door of the ancient building with Janie at his heels, and then clattered down the slate hall until he reached the great room of the Rolfe family hunting lodge. This large room with its massive stone fireplace had warmed many generations of hunters. Thomas had heard exciting tales about the Rolfe ancestors from Scandinavia. They too had been great hunters, and something about this manly room always felt like a homecoming to him. The walls were covered with trophy heads of stags and wild boars and even a massive bear. A great Rolfe family crest of roaring lions hung over the mantel, and it filled Thomas with pride each time he saw it.

Thomas longed to join the group of men gathered around the warming fire, but he knew his first duty, as always, was to greet Grandfather Rolfe. He walked over to the ancient leather chair of the slender old man, bowed quickly and said, "I am home, sir."

Grandfather simply nodded, but Thomas saw the twinkle in his eye. He knew the formalities and traditions of the Rolfe family were always underlined with kindness and genuine love.

"It has been a successful hunt," Grandfather announced. "Some of the men have already returned with the deer and pheasants. And we have esteemed guests! I see that you have already met Miss Poythress." Grandfather smiled at the young windblown rider by his side.

"Yes, sir," Thomas answered.

"And this is her honorable father, Colonel Poythress of the Virginia Company." Thomas reached out to shake the hand of the large gentleman who stepped forward and smiled.

"Pleased to make your acquaintance, sir," said Thomas with a respectful nod of his head.

"And of course, you recognize our old friend, Captain John Smith," Grandfather continued.

Thomas stood straight and tall as he politely reached out to grasp the big, familiar hand. But instead of a handshake, Thomas found himself caught up in a manly embrace that was anything but formal! Suddenly the entire room filled with hearty laughter, and Thomas joined in. John Smith pounded him on the back and roared, "Thomas, lad, you have grown as tall as the timber of the New World!"

Before long, they were all seated around the long oak table in the dining hall. Thomas sat between Janie and the captain, and across from him sat his older cousins, Edwin and Jacob, and his Uncle Edward. Platter after platter of steaming meat and salmon was set before them, and the hunting talk grew loud and boastful. Thomas glanced at the strange new utensil next to his plate. It was called a "fork" and Grandmother had insisted that they should use them to eat with, but no one touched the metal objects, except for Janie.

"I'm glad I got to come with Father on this trip," whispered Janie. "He hopes it will help prepare me for the outdoors, and for the day we will go to Jamestown."

He swallowed a gulp of cider and looked at her in surprise. "*You* are going to Jamestown?" he stammered. How could a mere girl travel across the ocean? He could hold his tongue no longer.

"Captain Smith," he blurted. "Are you returning to Jamestown?" The table grew silent as everyone leaned forward to listen.

"No, my boy, sadly the Company has not seen fit to re-appoint me to that fair land as of yet."

"Oh..." Thomas tried to conceal his disappointment. His only chance of joining Father seemed to vanish. It just wasn't fair.

"Although I am not returning to Jamestown, I have brought other good news. Would you like to tell him, Colonel Poythress?"

"Thank you, Captain." Janie's father stood and cleared his

throat as if he were going to make a speech. "The Virginia Company has received a special message from King James. The good King has remembered your mother with fondness, and therefore calls you to Court for a special audience with His Majesty!"

"An audience with the King!" exclaimed Grandfather. The guests broke into applause and congratulations.

"Oh, Pepsi," said Janie. "How wonderful!"

"Pepsi?" snickered Jacob from across the table. He elbowed Edwin and they both chuckled. Thomas tried to ignore them. Grandfather had explained that their teasing stemmed from jealousy. They resented Thomas' natural abilities to ride and hunt better than they. But sometimes, like now, Thomas' patience grew thin.

"Pepsi?" asked the captain and the cousins grew quiet. "Is that your Algonquin name?"

"Yes, sir," he answered. "My name is Thomas Pepsicanough."

"And do you know what that means?"

"No, sir. No one has ever told me."

"You must find out one day," declared Smith. "Algonquin names are filled with powerful meaning. No doubt this is the name of a great warrior." Grandfather nodded and the cousins said nothing.

"Yes, sir." Thomas straightened his back proudly. "I will learn what it means."

CHAPTER THREE

THE TOMAHAWK

Later that evening, Thomas sat alone in his room. He looked out the window and wondered if he would ever go to the Chesapeake. It just wasn't fair! A knock on his door interrupted his glum thoughts. He hoped it wasn't his cousins. He opened it just a crack, then wider when he saw the tall form standing there.

"Walk with me to the stable yard, young Pepsicanough. I have brought a gift for you," said Captain Smith.

Thomas hurried to match the brisk gate of John Smith as they strode out of the lodge. And as quickly as the man walked, he talked. He spoke of the Chesapeake and of his many adventures there. He told of friends and foes, both English and Indian.

"I have heard of the passing of your mother's father, Chief Powhatan," Captain Smith commented sadly.

"Yes," Thomas answered. "My father wrote to me about it."

"Your grandfather was a man to be respected. At his death, he left the leadership to his brother, Itopatin. But I have recently learned that Itopatin has also passed from the land of the living. Now your mother's old uncle, Opechcanough, is in command of the tribe. However, this is unwelcome news."

"Why, sir?" asked Thomas. "Do you know Opechcanough?"

"I'm afraid so. Chief Opech has always been bloodthirsty and ready to fight. I fear his leadership will bring trouble for both the Algonquin and the English."

Thomas thought of his father. Would he be in danger? He looked to Captain Smith, hoping for reassurance. After all, Opech would be his father's uncle by marriage; surely that must mean something. But the captain's brow remained creased in a deep frown.

He placed his hand on Thomas' shoulder. "You're no longer a child, Thomas. I thought it best to speak honestly with you."

"Yes, Captain, and I thank you for it."

"And it's because you're growing so quickly to manhood that I've brought you a man's gift."

Captain Smith reached into the bag that hung from his shoulder and pulled out a strange rectangular object with a short, smooth handle. Part of the object was encased in a beaded leather covering. He placed it reverently into Thomas' hands.

Thomas stroked the smooth wooden handle. The grain was as fine as silk. He carefully opened the case, then gasped when he pulled out, what he knew must be, an Algonquin tomahawk. He could tell, just by looking, that the blade was very sharp.

"This is a true treasure, young Pepsi," Captain Smith explained. "It probably came to your people in an expensive trade with the Hurons far to the north of the Chesapeake. It was given to me by your mother's favorite brother, Parahunt. He is as fine a warrior and friend as I have ever known and your mother loved him dearly."

Thomas held tight to the tomahawk, a lump growing in his throat. "Thank you, Captain." He gulped back the emotion he felt. He knew that Algonquins never cry.

"It's rightfully yours, lad. And you can thank me by learning to use it. If you use it right, you'll find Parahunt's tomahawk is a reliable weapon." Captain Smith patiently explained the technique for throwing the tomahawk. He had learned the skill from Pepsi's own people.

Before long, Janie came to watch as Thomas practiced throwing the tomahawk. She seated herself on a fence post without making any comments. Thomas decided he didn't mind her watching. But she better stay well out of the way!

After awhile, Thomas realized there was a definite art to hurling this strange weapon. He tried time and time again to throw the tomahawk. It was supposed to fly end over end until it stuck firmly in the wooden target. After an hour, his arm began to ache and throb from his numerous attempts. It seemed he would never figure it out!

Finally, he grew angry with himself. And instead of hurling the tomahawk toward the wooden target, he impulsively chucked it at an old hen walking through the stable yard. With a sickening swish, the tomahawk sliced right into the chicken's neck and completely lopped off its head. Thomas was stunned! He watched in horror as the headless body of the hen continued jerking about. He had seen this strange phenomena before when the cook would wring the chickens' necks, and the creatures would continue to move. And now this one was moving toward Janie. She screamed hysterically when the bloody feathery bundle ran straight at her.

Thomas lunged for the headless hen. "I'm sorry!" he shouted. "I didn't mean to do it! I didn't mean it!" He held tightly to the body of the hen until it finally went limp. Then he turned sheepishly to the captain. Thomas felt terrible. He never dreamed he could actually hit the old hen.

Suddenly this whole mishap seemed so ridiculous that he almost expected the captain to laugh at his misfortune. But Captain John Smith was not laughing. He wasn't even smiling.

"You will take that hen to the cooking room and pluck it and prepare it for our supper," Captain Smith said firmly.

"But I...I don't know how," Thomas protested.

"Then you will *learn* how." Captain Smith's voice grew louder. "An Algonquin is not like the English who will kill game and then waste it. You have killed this fowl, so now we must eat it." Thomas felt his face grow red. Even his copper-colored skin would not hide his humiliation.

Captain Smith continued to speak, more quietly now, but his tone remained serious. "This Algonquin tomahawk must never again be thrown on foolish impulse—at any living thing! If you don't understand this, then you are not worthy of Parahunt's weapon."

Thomas nodded seriously, then turned without another word, and headed for the cooking rooms back at the lodge. He knew he wasn't leaving for the Chesapeake today, but one day soon he would. And for now, he would take this opportunity to learn the ways of his people.

"More than anything," he whispered to himself as he plucked the white feathers from the chicken, "I want to be worthy of Parahunt's tomahawk. And I will not bring shame to my mother's people."

CHAPTER FOUR

THE KING'S GIFT

THE CARRIAGE BOUNCED and lurched along the cobblestone street as they finally headed into London. Thomas braced himself against the seat in an attempt to keep from smashing into Uncle Edward.

"Driver!" his uncle shouted up to the coachman. "Must you hit every broken cobblestone in the entire county?" Thomas was thankful that their week-long journey through cold, damp weather was almost over. He knew he hadn't been very good company for Uncle Edward. It wasn't that he meant to be sullen, but he was still so disappointed that Captain Smith hadn't offered to take him back to the Chesapeake to join Father.

It was time to cheer up, he told himself. And besides, a trip to London wasn't something one did everyday. Not only that, but he would actually *meet* the King of England today!

He tugged on his ruff, and wondered again why anyone should have to wear these tall, starched collars that seemed designed for torture. The collar was stiffened with wire to stand out above his velvet jacket. He supposed it was necessary to wear this thing to meet the King, but he felt half-strangled by it.

"I hate wearing these ridiculous dress duds!" Thomas groaned.

"Duds?" Uncle Edward asked. "What in the world does *that* word mean?"

"It's a new slang word for clothes, Uncle," Thomas explained. "The writer Shakespeare called clothes duds."

"Slang words! They're as troublesome as the blasted new forks we're expected to eat with," Uncle Edward complained. "Just be careful you don't say such things before King James! Be a credit to your grandparents, Thomas."

"I wish they'd been well enough to join us," said Thomas. "But at least they prepared me. All I've heard around Heacham lately is court manners, court manners!"

"Well, remember the most important courtesy is that the King is always right. And the only reply to give a king is a simple yes."

Thomas nodded soberly. He thought he could remember that. He pulled on the stiff collar again. If only he didn't have to wear these silly duds! The rhythm of the bumpy road changed, and Thomas looked out in time to see that they were crossing London Bridge.

The sounds and smells of the crowded city seeped into the closed carriage. Thomas opened his window curtain wider to see the narrow, winding streets. The streets were crowded with hundreds of colorful vendor carts. It was market day in London, and it appeared that everyone was out shopping.

They passed a group of spice vendors and Thomas leaned his head out to inhale the exotic aromas. He caught the fragrance of sweet cinnamon and pungent curry. Next he saw fabric merchants with rainbow stacks of silks, brocades, and velvets.

Thomas' stomach rumbled as they passed food stalls. And his mouth watered to see piles of sweet-smelling pastries, and strings of sausages hanging from a vendor's rack.

London was such an exciting place! He had only been here once since Mother's death. He wished they could stop to watch the dancing muzzled bears, or perhaps buy a stringed puppet to take home. But Thomas knew better than to ask. This was an important day. They hadn't come all this way just to dally.

Finally they reached the rise of road which overlooked the Tower of London. Uncle Edward pounded his walking cane on the roof of the coach, and the driver immediately halted the carriage. Thomas and Uncle Edward both got out to stretch their legs.

Thomas looked up at the tall fortress that also housed the ancient prison. The dark, massive stone walls seemed almost to echo with the cries of prisoners from times gone by. Members of royalty, lords and ladies, and hundreds of common folk had known the heaviness of the prison chains. Thomas had heard gruesome stories of the torture rack, and that many had been beheaded in the Tower.

Thomas turned away from that sight and gazed upon the River Thames. There, small boats ferried cargo to and from the sailing ships at the docks. He wondered if Janie Poythress and her family might be getting ready to set sail for Jamestown at this very moment. *How lucky they were!* He tried not to envy them. But right now he felt as if he were doomed to an eternal wait in England—and *that* seemed like a prison sentence!

Thomas and his uncle climbed back into the coach, and didn't get out again until they passed out of London and reached the palace of Hampton Court. Although he had been here once as a small child, he was still amazed at the size of the grand castle. They were met by a tall, sober page who escorted them to a long impressive hall. There they were instructed to wait until the King requested their presence in his private receiving chambers.

Thomas tried not to stare at the unusual assortment of people who also waited in the long waiting room. There were elegantly dressed lords and ladies, colorful business merchants, and foreigners wearing unusual clothing and conversing in unrecognizable languages.

Even a group of several American natives were gathered! They wore long feathers and brightly-colored ceremonial paint. And although they looked somewhat familiar, there was also something strange about them. What tribe could *they* be from?

A plump elderly woman edged her way toward Thomas and Uncle Edward. Behind her, like a peacock's tail, trailed yards of purple satin. Her powdered wig was piled high and her thick neck was ringed with jewels. She cleared her throat and peered curiously at the two of them through an ornate monocle.

"I recognize you, sir," she finally said to Uncle Edward. *"You* are the brother of my friend, John Rolfe of Jamestown. I am the Lady De La Ware. My husband was once the governor of Jamestown."

"Yes, Lady De La Ware." Uncle Edward bowed. "I remember meeting you at the court balls when you were hosting the Princess Pocahontas. May I present my nephew—"

"I see clearly who this is!" she interrupted and turned to Thomas with an enormous smile. *"You* are the son of Pocahontas and John Rolfe. I knew it the minute I saw you! You have your mother's glowing skin, her lovely dark eyes, even her strong, handsome features. I knew you when you were a baby!" Lady De

La Ware bubbled over him like a doting grandmother. He glanced around uncomfortably. He hoped she wasn't going to pinch his cheek, or something equally embarrassing.

"I last saw you when I accompanied your mother to the prison in the Tower of London," she continued. "And she insisted on bringing you with us."

"My mother and I visited the Tower?"

"Yes, my dear. We called on Sir Percy, the Earl of Northumberland. The Earl's younger brother was a friend of your mother's back in Jamestown. We were escorted into the Tower by Sir Walter Raleigh."

"Sir Walter Raleigh knew my mother!" Thomas exclaimed. "Why, he was the greatest soldier of our time!"

"Yes, Thomas, Sir Walter greatly admired your mother. And it was the prisoner, Sir Percy, who set those fine pearls that Powhatan gave your mother. The dear man did it in his tiny workroom at the prison. You know, she wore those lovely earrings in the portraits your father had painted."

Thomas would have to take another look at those earrings when he got home. To think, he had actually met Sir Walter Raleigh and Sir Percy! It was something to be proud of, even if he had been just a toddler at the time.

Lady De La Ware lowered her voice and leaned closer to Uncle Edward. "I don't know what you're here for," she said. "But I can tell you, our good King James is not long for this world. They bleed him daily and he seldom leaves his bed." She paused for a moment and glanced at Thomas, then she continued in a hushed tone.

"Of course the country will be thrown into turmoil when he dies. I just hope *none of us* find ourselves imprisoned in the

Tower." Thomas wondered what she meant, but before he could ask she embraced him in an almost suffocating hug and turned to leave. The great width of her skirt was braced with rows of wires, and almost knocked him off balance.

He managed to mumble, "Thank you, ma'am," and gave her a slight bow. At first, he had been put off by this busy, chattering woman, but now he was glad to have met her. Sir Walter Raleigh—indeed!

"Masters Edward and Thomas Rolfe," announced the page in a deep, formal voice. Thomas straightened his ruff and followed his uncle into a bright room. He glanced nervously around to see reflective mirrored walls and furnishings trimmed in gold leaf. And before them, on an elaborate throne-like bed, reclined a very old and very pale man.

Thomas bowed himself low to the floor. He remembered how many times he had practiced this back at Heacham. He hoped he had done it right.

"Come here, young Rolfe, son of Pocahontas. Let me look at you," the old King commanded. Thomas stepped forward. His heart pounded and his palms grew damp.

"Queen Anne and I received your mother in this very room. Did you know that?"

"Yes, Your Majesty," he answered carefully.

"Pocahontas was well loved in this court. Her ways were gentle, her words were gracious, and my dear Queen Anne found her faith inspiring."

"Yes, Your Majesty," Thomas answered with a solemn smile. Once again, he felt proud to be the son of the Princess Pocahontas.

"She and her people created quite a lasting impression here.

In fact," he went on, "members of the royal household often dress up for our masquerade balls as Algonquin natives." He turned his head toward the massive carved door. "Page!" he commanded. "Bring in those artisans in their costumes for our next masquerade ball. I want the son of Pocahontas to see them."

The page flung wide the door and motioned with a wave of his arm. Within minutes, the strange-looking group of Indians trooped in. So, they were *not* natives at all. They were actually English men and women dressed up in costume!

Thomas spotted pale legs and freckled arms standing out strangely wherever the native skins and feathers parted. And beneath the dark black wigs showed bits of fair English hair.

"Well, what do you think?" King James smiled at him. "Do these look like good Algonquins?" Thomas paused uncomfortably. How could he honestly say 'yes, your Majesty'? Uncle Edward looked at Thomas sternly.

"I...I don't know, Your Highness," he stammered. "I have not seen an Algonquin since the death of my mother."

"Of course, of course..." the King spoke slowly, and with a flick of his hand he waved the costume makers away. He looked at Thomas with sadness, as if he might understand how it felt to lose a mother.

There was a long pause before the King began to speak. "I tire quickly these days. I must get on with the reason I have called you."

"Yes, Your Majesty," Thomas answered.

"In this very palace of Hampton Court I authorized the common man's translation of the Holy Bible. Did you know that?" he asked.

"No, Your Majesty."

"In 1604, I called a meeting to settle arguments between the Church of England and the Puritans. We were not successful. However, at that time, a Puritan leader, John Reynolds, asked if a new version of the Bible might be produced. I believed this idea to be divine and therefore funded the undertaking. I assigned this work to fifty scholars of every religion, and the first books were produced here, by the King's Printer."

"It was a great undertaking, Majesty," Thomas said. He tried not to squirm or tug on his collar. But he wondered what any of this had to do with him.

"Yes, my boy. Queen Anne told your mother of this new Bible. And your mother asked to have one of these Bibles to take back to her father's people. But in those days, no volumes were completed. The Queen had no book to give to your mother. Therefore we promised to send one to her as soon as it was available." The King sighed. "And then we heard of her untimely death."

Thomas swallowed hard.

"I decided it would be pleasing to see the son of Pocahontas. Now I want to present you with the Bible requested by your mother."

An attendant brought an elaborately stamped and gilded leather volume and placed the heavy book in Thomas' arms. The cover was soft and the smell reminded him of his grandfather's library. His fingers traced the gold lettering. He opened the cover and read the inscription: *For the Son of the Princess Pocahontas.*

"Perhaps *you* will take this Bible to your mother's people," said the King.

Thomas tried to speak, but no sound came out. His heart felt warmed with such a gift.

"Your Majesty," Uncle Edward said, "young Thomas and I are grateful. We thank you on behalf of the entire family."

Thomas finally formed the words, "Thank you, Your Majesty." He trembled as he bent to kiss the ring on the old King's finger.

Then with a wave of the monarch's hand, the audience was over, and Thomas found himself dismissed from the presence of King James.

As they walked from the palace Thomas looked straight ahead. He hugged the heavy book tight to his chest with both arms wrapped around it. When their carriage rumbled away from the palace, he still clutched the Bible on his lap and held it like it was a chest full of valuable gold.

In the past few weeks he had been given two treasures. First, Parahunt's mighty tomahawk. And now, the Bible which the King had promised to his mother.

King James had said that this Bible was to be taken to his mother's people. In fact, the wise King had even suggested that Thomas might take it. Wasn't that almost like a decree? Surely, Grandfather would allow him to return to the Chesapeake to join his father now.

CHAPTER FIVE

THE MASSACRE

THE JOURNEY HOME to Heacham Hall took almost a week by coach, but Thomas enjoyed the trip this time. For one thing, the weather was mild, but more than that, Thomas was elated over the hope that this precious Bible might provide just the excuse for him to make the trip to the Chesapeake!

They made many stops along the way, taking each meal at a different country inn. The food was mostly soup and tough bread, but they met interesting characters, and heard bits of news from all corners of the land. And when fellow travelers discovered that Thomas was returning from a private audience with the King, they would lift their tumblers high in a toast, and offer him a free drink of cider ale. Many of them had heard of the Princess Pocahontas. Thomas was surprised to learn that his mother was becoming something of a legend.

Finally, Thomas and Uncle Edward reached the village of King's Lynn near Heacham. There, they claimed their own horses from the caretaker at the Fox and Hound pub. Thomas carefully packed the large Bible into his saddle pack. Then he stroked Moco's soft nose, and climbed eagerly into the saddle.

"You ride on ahead, Nephew!" Uncle Edward called. How did his uncle guess that Thomas longed to race Moco across the fields and straight toward home?

Thomas cried, "Yeeesssss!" and with one tap of the heel, Moco lunged forward. It felt great to race with the wind again! And he could hardly wait to see his grandparents—he had so much to tell them! Then he would sit down and write a long letter to his father, describing all about his visit with King James, and the amazing Bible that he must deliver to the Chesapeake.

The big black horse's hooves made a wonderful clattering sound as they cantered down the old roadway. At last, they reached the Heacham borders and he jumped Moco over the thick hedge and pounded cross-country through the lush meadows. Moco easily cleared stone walls and rickety wooden fences. He was a born jumper.

"On, boy!" Thomas yelled. "Fly!" Finally, Moco splashed through the stream near the lodge and Thomas slowed him down to a trot. As they drew near the large house, Thomas looked about for cousins or servants, but no one ran out to meet him. Usually, the massive old two-story house bustled with activity. Surely the family was alerted to their return.

He turned Moco into the side yard, then hopped down and looped the reins around the iron hitching post. With extreme care, he pulled the prized Bible from his saddlebag and hugged it in his arms. This was great; he would surprise them! What fun to see their faces!

He tiptoed down the long hallway, but the grand house felt strangely quiet. No smiling doorman greeted him. No servants bantered and laughed from the kitchen. At last he saw a serving woman through an open doorway, but she looked at him with stricken eyes. What was going on here?

He entered the library to find Uncle Edward's wife with another aunt. Their eyes were swollen and red, as if they'd been crying.

"Is it Grandfather?" Thomas pleaded.

"No, he is not ill, dear," his aunt answered.

"Then, dear Grandmother, is she all right?" Thomas pressed for an answer, but this time the aunts only stepped away so he could clearly see that both grandparents were seated in the library. Still, the room seemed filled with a cloud of darkness.

He hurried close to Grandmother. She was huddled in her rocker, her head buried in her hands, muttering, "My son...oh, my son...." Grandfather sat silently on the edge of his chair. He stooped forward on his ancient cane as if a great weight pressed upon his frail shoulders. He did not weep, but his whole body quivered with emotion.

"Come close, lad," Grandfather urged in a quiet voice. Thomas forced his legs to move forward, but they felt like two wooden poles. In his heart he knew. Something was wrong. Terribly wrong.

"Oh, Thomas," Grandfather moaned. "This day we have received terrible news from Jamestown."

Thomas stood frozen. This had to do with Father. A chill ran from his scalp to his toes.

"There has been a massacre." Grandfather's voice shook as his words tumbled out. "It happened on the 22nd day of March. We just this morning received the news. Over 350 of the settlers have been slaughtered." He shook his head with a blank stare. "Over 350. And the bloody attack was led by your mother's own uncle—that cursed Chief Opech."

"And my father?" Thomas could barely gasp the words.

"Your father, my dear son, has perished. He was slain at Henrico, defending the home of the minister."

For a long moment, Thomas could not respond. He could not seem to feel this thing, this darkness which had come upon them. The aunts at the doorway now wept aloud with Grandmother, but Thomas could not utter a sound. How could this happen? And on the very day when he had returned home so excited about taking the gift of his mother's Bible to the Chesapeake?

Grandfather reached a trembling hand out to touch Thomas' fingers. And in that instant, Thomas broke.

He turned and dashed from the room. On, up the wide stairway, he ran until he reached his own bedroom chambers. He slammed the door and leaned against it, his heart pounding with pain. He looked down to the Bible still in his hands. *For his mother's people?* He lifted the heavy book and hurled it against the wall. He watched it smash to the floor with a hollow thud, falling limply open into a heap of pages and leather.

He pounded his fists against his bookcase, then dumped all the books to the floor. He kicked and smashed all his possessions, even his prized collection of toy soldiers. He ripped the heavy damask bed curtains from his poster bed and threw them to the floor. He jerked paintings from the walls. His fury and rage went on and on.

He did not cry.

"I am preparing a great place for you here," Father had written to him. Every single day of his life, Thomas had looked forward to the time when he would join his father in the Chesapeake. Now that day would never come.

He had lost his mother. Now his father was gone forever, too. And slain by an Algonquin! Thomas' own blood relative. All of Captain Smith's worries about the evil Chief Opech had proven true.

How could the world be so cruel? He wanted to feel sorrow, but all he felt was wave after wave of anger. He remembered his talk with Janie Poythress, and how he had foolishly told her that he would return to the Chesapeake and become a Chief in that New World.

*   *   *

Finally night crept into his room. He knew he had been alone for hours, and that he should go down to Grandfather and Grandmother—they needed him now more than ever. But he knew he would find no comfort for his own heart.

He picked the King James Bible from the floor, then walked over to his storage chest. He opened the lid and pushed the Bible deep inside until he reached the bottom. And there he buried it, down under the box holding his mother's pearl earrings, beneath Parahunt's tomahawk, and his father's letters and all the other treasures of his lifetime. He silently vowed to never open that book again. He would never take it to his mother's people now.

He had always been so proud to be an Algonquin—a grandson of the mighty Powhatan. But the people of the Chesapeake were savages. He wanted no part of them, not now, not ever.

"I am not Algonquin," Thomas spat through clenched teeth. "I will stay in England, and I will never, never return to the land of my birth!"

CHAPTER SIX

CAMBRIDGE

"PULL, THOMAS, PULL! Row harder! You're winning!" From the river bank, his classmates screamed encouragement. But Thomas didn't look up. Instead he squinted his eyes and continued to focus mind and muscle into each strong stroke. As a teenager, his arms were already built like a man's. He pulled against the water with perfect rhythm and the small skiff cut smoothly through the river. He was seated backwards, in order to put the power of his whole body into each motion.

Small pockets of fog hung low on the Cam River and each time Thomas' skiff burst through the mist, his friends' cheers grew louder. One by one, he inched past the skiffs manned by boys from other schools. Finally he crossed under the shadow of the ancient bridge of Cambridge to wild cheers and cries of triumph.

"Thomas wins!" shouted the crowd. With arms still shaking, Thomas gulped for air as he managed a broad grin. His school friends pulled him from the boat and happily pounded him on the back.

"This is the first time our college has won the river race in years," exclaimed his friend Andrew. "You're a school hero! Tonight in chapel, you'll receive a medal!"

Thomas and his friends marched victoriously up the hill. As they passed the ivy-covered buildings, a young professor joined in their procession. Professor Joshua Featherstone was one of Thomas' favorite teachers—a brilliant man who could make even the hardest lines of Greek and Latin understandable.

"Well, done, Master Rolfe," the professor said. "You are the pride of the college, and a natural leader among men today!"

"Thank you, sir."

"And," Professor Featherstone went on, his eyes twinkling, "I noticed quite a few young ladies from the village lined the river banks to cheer such a handsome young sportsman."

"That's right, sir," laughed Andrew. "Thomas could go courting any girl he chose."

Thomas felt the heat of embarrassment on his face. He hoped it didn't show through his dark copper skin.

"And why don't you go courting any of these pretty village girls?" Professor Featherstone teased.

"I don't know, sir," Thomas shrugged. "I never know what to say when I'm with a girl."

Featherstone laughed. "Well, don't worry, I'll not tease you anymore. Now you must hurry on to your dinner. You need good food and rest for the other competitions tomorrow. I understand that you're a great wrestler, as well as a boatman."

"He is!" blurted Andrew. "Thomas is strong enough to wrestle the bears that put on those shows in London!"

Thomas punched Andrew in the arm to quiet him down. He was tired of all this attention. Besides, if they kept talking like this, it might come out that he had already agreed to wrestle a bear at the upcoming Spring Fair near Heacham.

It was all because of a silly dare from his cousin. Of course, the bear would be only a young one, but Thomas didn't want any of his Cambridge friends to show up and think of him as a crazy country roughneck who could be dared into such foolishness.

The group cut across an emerald green playing field bordered with flowering trees. Nearby, the gray towers and red brick buildings of Cambridge rose over the fields like monuments to the great men who had studied there. Thomas liked to imagine what it was like for writers like Chaucer and Spenser, or the great thinkers like Sir Francis Bacon, when they had been students here. He walked through the ancient stone of the quadrangle and pounded up the stairs to his tiny third-story room.

He liked school, and he liked being called a leader. Especially in a school where so many of the students were sons of lords. And school kept him busy. So busy that he didn't have time to think about his father's horrible death. He was glad to lose himself in study and sports. And sometimes he could almost forget who he was.

He hurried to clean up and dress for dinner. Then he pulled on the required wool serge cap and gown. Some of his friends were sons of noblemen. They had to wear robes made of silk and caps of velvet.

Although the Rolfes were gentlemen, they were not nobility. But Thomas was glad he didn't need to lead that stuffy kind of life. He slammed his door and clattered down the stairs. He was starving!

In the dining hall he found his proper place at the long, candlelit table called a "fellows table." This was where "gentleman commoners" were seated: students who attended school on scholarship, but paid for living expenses. Of course, the sons of noblemen had their own special tables. And on the lowest level, eating humbly, were the poor students who were admitted not because of their names but because of their abilities. About sixty undergraduates were gathered for this formal dinner.

Thomas looked up at the polished wooden walls of the dining hall. It was interesting to see the portraits of all the great men who had studied at this college. He wondered if his portrait might ever hang there, but he didn't think so.

Tonight, after grace was said by a tutor, everyone was served a large portion of the new food brought back from South America. It was a vegetable called "potato". Some of the boys complained, but Thomas loved potatoes; he mashed them with his fork and sprinkled them heavily with salt.

As the students devoured their dinner, the headmaster climbed the few steps to the speaking pulpit in the corner of the room.

"The results of today's skiff races have been glorious for our college!" he exclaimed. "We especially want to congratulate the young man who won the final competition—our fellow from Norfolk, Master Thomas Rolfe!" The boys clapped and stomped their feet, and from the faculty table, Professor Featherstone beamed at Thomas.

"Tomorrow's wrestling competition will be the final sport in our spring event," the elderly speaker went on. "But I have to announce that following the wrestling tournament, we must make a change in the spring schedule." The old dean paused and the room grew quiet.

"I was informed this morning that two of our students have been taken to their homes because of illness. A serious illness that bears a resemblance to the symptoms of the Plague."

Many of the students gasped, including Thomas. This was a very sobering announcement. He knew from the loss of his own mother how quickly death could come.

"The leaders and I have no choice but to dismiss the college for at least a month," the dean announced to the hushed crowd. "You all know that only four years ago the Plague swept through our halls like wildfire, taking the lives of half our students. We were forced to adjourn for that entire year. By making this decision to dismiss our classes early, we hope to save many lives. If all goes well, we plan to call you back to your studies in June."

The roomful of young men finished their meal quietly. The dismissal of class and release to go home would normally be reason to celebrate, but the shadow of the Plague hung over them all.

Everyone knew when the Plague began, there was no stopping it. The dean and faculty had found the only answer. They all must leave, and leave soon.

LIGHTNING

"COME IN, THOMAS, come close!" Grandfather called from the great hall. Thomas peeled off his wet cloak and smiled. It was good to see Grandfather comfortably seated by the fireside.

"Give your soaking coat to the serving girl, lad. And come warm yourself by the fire. I worry this cold spring rain might cause a chill to weaken you." Grandfather slowly pushed himself to his feet and enclosed him in a firm embrace. He then held him at arm's length and peered into Thomas' face with concern.

"We heard the news that your school had to close. Do you feel you have any signs of the Plague? Do you think that we should call for our physician to come and bleed you?" Thomas knew that, since the death of his father in Jamestown, Grandfather greatly feared losing any more loved ones.

"No, dear sir, I'm sure I have no infection." Thomas helped the old man back to his chair. "I am strong and well. And look, I've brought you medals that I won in the sporting events at college. Here is the one for the boat race, and this one is for wrestling."

"Boating and wrestling. You are a champion! But I think that

I could still beat you at falconry!" Grandfather's eyes twinkled.

"Yes, sir!" Thomas agreed. No one compared to Grandfather when it came to training hunting birds.

Thomas planned to enjoy this unexpected break from school's hard schedule of study. He had missed his great thoroughbred, Moco, and the next morning, he saddled up the stallion and sped across the fields of his childhood home. Somehow being at Heacham brought back more memories of his father. Here he had dreamed about what it would be like to join him in the Chesapeake. Now those dreams must die!

He urged Moco on up to the rugged country. They soared over rock fences and high hedges with no particular destination. Thomas didn't care where they rode. He only wanted to ride fast and hard; maybe that way he could escape the anger that seemed to chase him ever since his father's murder. But no matter where he went or how hard he tried, the quiet anger clung to him like a stubborn shadow.

Finally even Moco grew tired and his pace slowed. Thomas let up on the rein and allowed the tired horse to head back down to the manor. He led the lathered horse into the stable yard. He felt ashamed for running Moco so hard, and offered to cool him down, but the groomsman wouldn't hear of it.

As he entered the house, he was met by Grandfather. "Thomas, why don't you take one of my hunting birds out? I haven't been able to work with them lately, but they need to be kept in training. I know we don't use them much anymore, but a good hunting falcon can keep its owner from starving."

Thomas went gladly to the mews—the bird shelter which was near the stable. He chose the falcon, Loch Lightning. The bird was named for a Scottish lake where Grandfather had found the young peregrine falcon in a storm. Left for dead by a high-land clansman, the falcon had suffered a broken wing. But Grandfather had patiently set the wing and waited for it to heal.

Thomas carried the great bird on his arm into the sunlight. Smoothly, he slipped the hood from Lightning and the bird soared high into the sky. Thomas watched her with admiration. She was not only a devoted hunter, but she was lean and power-ful, and as quick as the lightning of the north.

The next morning Thomas announced that he wanted to try something new with Lightning. The falcon had been trained as a "rooker", a bird that caught its game on the ground. But Thomas believed that Lightning was so clever that she could be retrained to catch game birds as they flew through the air.

"That would be impossible," insisted Grandfather. "A falcon can only be trained for one technique or the other—not both! And Lightning finished her training years ago."

But despite Grandfather's opinion, Thomas decided to fol-low his hunch. Day after day, he worked patiently with Lightning. He began to train her just as if she had never been trained at all. He knew that when falcons were very young, train-ers would often stay in the mews day and night. The goal was for a falcon to become so relaxed that it would even sleep while roosting on the arm of its owner. Thomas decided to start spend-ing the night in the mews. And after only a couple of nights, she finally slept on his shoulder!

Now, he felt sure the great falcon trusted him enough to allow him to take her the next step. He tied a line to one of her claws, and the other end was attached to the cadge perch. This was to keep her from soaring high into the sky when he pointed his finger in the hunt signal.

Thomas had designed a decoy with feathers and wings from a large grouse, and tied it to a long rope. Now he slipped Lightning's hood off, but instead of signaling for her to soar, he began to swing the decoy around and around over his head.

Lightning took off for the sky, planning to hover above the decoy, then to hurl down and pin it to the ground. But instead, she hit the end of the restraining line and was jerked backward. She landed clumsily on the perch, confused and stunned. She cocked her head and watched Thomas. He just continued to quietly twirl the decoy in the air above his head.

Again and again, Lightning took off, heading straight upward. And again and again she was snapped back toward the ground and her perch. Finally, she just sat very still and focused her sharp eyes upon the swirling decoy, following every wide circle without blinking.

Then suddenly, and as quick as her name, Lightning swooped forward and snatched the decoy in her deadly clutches—right in midair! Thomas couldn't help but give a whoop of victory, but Lightning wasn't disturbed. She finally understood. There was some prey that could only be caught while in flight. Thomas couldn't wait to show Grandfather.

That afternoon Grandfather hobbled out of the house and leaned against the fence in the stable yard. He watched in wonder while Thomas led Lightning in a demonstration.

"Beats everything I've ever seen." The old gentleman shook his head in amazement as Lightning captured the decoy in midair again. "You really have retrained her, Thomas! Your way with God's creatures is indeed a wonder, my lad."

At last, Lightning returned to her perch and Thomas slipped the leather hood over her head. He stroked her smooth feathers and smiled. This was a proud moment. Even better than winning the boat race. But suddenly a shadow crossed Grandfather's face and a deep frown creased his brow.

"Oh, Thomas." Grandfather spoke the words slowly, as if they caused him physical pain. "How I wish I could give you Lightning. You certainly deserve her. But you know Jacob is your elder cousin, and long ago I gave his father my word that Lightning would go to Jacob."

Thomas knew of the promise to cousin Jacob, and he suspected that Jacob had asked for the bird just because he knew she was special to Thomas. Everyone knew that Jacob didn't care a whit about hunting birds.

"Don't worry, Grandfather," said Thomas. "Before Jacob left for sea, he said I could have the chance to earn Lightning from him."

"Splendid!" Grandfather said. "Splendid!" His face lit up and he turned to walk back to the manor house.

Thomas carried Lightning back to the mews, and tried to recall exactly how Jacob had talked him into this crazy scheme. It had all started last Christmas. After the family dinner, the cousins played games, and Jacob became irked when Thomas won an arm wrestling match.

"Well, Thomas, since everyone thinks you're so strong," Jacob teased, "why don't you prove it by wrestling a bear at the country fair this spring? I'll bet you're not *that* strong."

"That's a splendid idea," chimed in Jacob's younger brother, Edwin. "You always act like you're so brave and tough."

"That's a stupid dare," Thomas answered, turning away. He was used to Edwin and Jacob's needling, and knew how to ignore them.

"Maybe," Jacob grinned with meanness. "But I'd be willing to make a wager of something important, something you *really* want...."

"Nothing you have could be that great," Thomas said.

"I'd be willing to bet the *falcon* that Grandfather promised to me...."

Thomas turned and stared at Jacob. Surely he was still joking. "You'd be willing to bet Lightning?"

"Sure. Edwin, you're my witness. Right now, I bet the falcon Lightning that you aren't brave enough or strong enough to wrestle a bear."

And Thomas had accepted.

Now as he settled Lightning in the mews, he still thought she was worth it. He spoke soothingly to her. "You're a good bird, Lightning. You did something today that even Grandfather thought was impossible."

He still felt amazed that she had trusted him enough to allow him to retrain her. But she understood him. She *had* to belong to him, and not to Jacob. He laid his hand gently upon her back. "I may be a fool, Lightning," he whispered. "But I am willing to face a bear in order to win you!"

CHAPTER EIGHT

FOOLISH DARE

THE SATURDAY OF THE SPRING FAIR dawned sunny and clear, and Thomas was ready to face the day. "I want to be the first one at the Fair today," he announced at breakfast. Grandfather laughed at his eagerness but he didn't know about Jacob's dare. Thomas hoped to get the dreadful task finished before any of his relatives arrived at the Fair. He didn't want anyone to stop him.

Thomas rode Moco the few miles to the Spring Fair meadow. Already the booths that lined the green meadow were buzzing with activity. On a small rise on the edge of the meadow stood a tall maypole. A worker had climbed to the top to attach the long colorful streamers. Thomas knew that the prettiest girls of the village would perform the maypole dance. But he had more pressing concerns right now.

He saw that the men who ran the sporting competitions were busy, too. Everyone was getting ready for a great day. Thomas led Moco over to the temporary stable. The big horse grew edgy and nervous, as the other horses stomped and neighed. Thomas knew they could smell the bear penned up nearby.

He walked toward the temporary ring, centered in the wide meadow. Thomas sucked in a deep breath when he saw the grunting brown bear pacing. This year's animal was no cub. He stared at the animal in disbelief. It was much larger than the bears that had been at the Fair in the past. Thomas groaned and walked toward the keeper, he might as well get it over—

"Thomas!" called a girl's voice. "Thomas Pepsicanough Rolfe!" He stopped in his tracks and turned to see who it was. Only one girl ever called him by his Algonquin name. That was Janie Poythress! But when he turned he saw a beautiful young lady in a wide bonnet and an emerald green dress. She wore a garland of fresh spring flowers around her neck. He looked closer—and the reddish curls and sparkling eyes gave her away. It *was* Janie!

"Do you recognize me?" she asked, smiling.

"Not at first," Thomas answered honestly. "But now I do, Janie." He bowed. "I'm surprised to see you here; I thought you'd gone with your father to Jamestown several years back."

"My father went to Jamestown," she explained. "We were all ready, but just as my family was about to sail, we heard about the horrible massacre led by Chief Opech. Father decided to continue alone. But I still hope he'll send for us to join him there someday." Suddenly she paused and he saw the sympathy in her eyes. "Oh, Pepsi, I was so very, very sorry to hear the news about your father during that massacre."

He nodded, and gazed at the ground. "I will *never* go to Jamestown now," he spoke quietly but firmly. "I have no desire to *ever* see the Chesapeake."

She looked truly surprised, and Thomas suspected she was keeping her opinions to herself. But after a long moment she spoke. "Well, I am very lucky to meet you here this morning. You see, I came to the Fair with my aunt, and she insists that I dance the maypole. But I need a partner. Thomas Pepsi Rolfe, would you please be my partner so that I do not have to choose a stranger?" She smiled up at him. She looked so pretty in the golden morning sun. And to his surprise he wanted to say yes.

"I…uh…no, Janie, I can't be your partner today." He forced the bitter words out.

He instantly knew that her feelings were hurt. The sunny smile disappeared and it was plain to see she was embarrassed for asking. Of course, he could give no reason. How could he explain that he'd accepted a foolish bet to wrestle a bear in order to win a bird? This was a rowdy event for the rough village boys—not something a Rolfe would participate in.

"Well then, I must be going." She tilted her chin up and the warmth was gone from her eyes. If only there was some way to make her understand.

"I would be most glad to accompany you in the maypole dance," an all-too-familiar voiced piped up. Thomas turned to see cousin Edwin standing behind him. He must have come to the Fair early to see if Thomas would follow through on Jacob's dare!

Edwin tossed a haughty look to Thomas, then smiled at Janie. "It's been ages since I've seen you, Miss Jane Poythress. But I well remember your delightful visit to the hunting lodge." His cousin might have been gangly and homely, but he always knew the right thing to say to girls.

"Well, thank you, Edwin. Thank you for your courtesy," Janie answered, taking his arm. The two turned to walk away, and Thomas felt like a pot ready to boil! He was not only furious with Edwin, but also with himself. Would he ever see Janie again? And even if he did, would she speak to him?

When they were well out of sight, he slipped through the growing crowd to find the manager of the bear pen. He was in a fighting mood now!

"I want to wrestle the bear," he announced. "I want to be the first of the day."

The tough-looking manager eyed him up and down. He looked almost as tough as the animal he cared for. Finally, he nodded and said, "Reckon you'll do. But gentlemen don't usually care for this challenge. You must have some mighty big gambling debts."

"I do not want the prize money. But I do have something to prove."

"All right, boy," the burly man shrugged. "It's yer skin, not mine. There's only one rule—ya must stay in the pen with the bear for a full five minutes. And yer the first customer of the day—she'll be fresh and mean!"

Thomas took off his coat and handed it to the manager. Underneath his breath, he whispered, "God, help me…God help me," over and over. Then he remembered a prayer that Professor Featherstone had taught: "God, help me to *think.*"

As he walked toward the pen, a crowd began to gather. They were mostly good-natured farmers who'd come to the Fair for a welcome break from their hard work. But Thomas heard a few of them taunt and jeer. They joked loudly about how bear wrestling was for full-grown farm-hands, fresh from the pub— that any young gentleman wanting to wrestle a bear must be a fool.

Thomas climbed up the sturdy fence and swung his legs inside the ring. The bear began to circle and growl. Her mouth was muzzled in a steel cage, but her claws were long and lethal-looking. Thomas knew that a bear this big only needed to give him one strong hug to crush all of his ribs. He breathed another desperate prayer and slipped into the ring. He cautiously circled the animal, always facing her—the same way he would face a fellow wrestler at school. The circling went on and on. And Thomas hoped it might last for five minutes.

Suddenly the bear lunged forward. But Thomas was quick. He jumped sideways and rolled out of her reach in a fast somersault. The bear lunged again and again. And each time Thomas somersaulted out of the way. Soon the crowd began to cheer. "Hey, watch this boy!" someone shouted. "He's a real athlete!"

"It's young Rolfe!" yelled a neighbor. Thomas sensed that more people were gathering around the pen to watch the contest, but he didn't allow his eyes to leave the bear. He wiped sweat from his brow and continued to focus on his growling opponent.

This time the bear attempted a different tactic. She reared up on her hind legs and walked toward him, swinging her paws like a boxer. Once again Thomas lunged sideways, but before he could roll the bear caught him with her paw and flung him across the ring. He gasped to regain the wind that was knocked out of him, as he stared up at her snarling face just inches from his. She growled and smacked him again and again.

Thomas fought to keep a clear head and remain conscious. But he felt the bear's claws slice through his cambric shirt, and cut a gaping strip across his chest. He knew he was bleeding badly, and his rib cage burned with each breath. *God, help me to think.*

A memory came to him—something he'd seen a farmer do

once before in the bear ring. The big man had rolled into a ball and played dead. It was Thomas' only hope. He tucked his head and legs in and wrapped his arms tightly around his knees, and prayed that the five minutes would soon end.

Each time the bear slapped at him, Thomas rolled. And after the force of each blow, he kept as still as if he were dead. Three more times the bear slapped him, but each time Thomas remained perfectly still. Finally, the she-bear grew bored and slunk away. Thomas watched through half-closed eyes, afraid even to breathe. The bear turned her head to the crowd and shook it back and forth as if to say that she was done. The crowd was jeering.

Then, with the bear's back to him, Thomas took a deep and painful breath and soundlessly stood. And before the bear could turn, he leaped onto her hairy back and clung for dear life. The crowd went wild, cheering, "Rolfe! Rolfe!" He grabbed a hold onto the chain that was attached to the muzzle and wrapped his long legs around the bear's mid-section. The surprised bear bucked and swung about in wild circles. She even rolled over once, but Thomas hung on tight. At least she could not get him with those horrible claws. This seemed the safest place to be—if he could just hold on.

"Get out of the ring, Thomas Pepsi!" He heard a girl's voice scream. "Please come out of the ring!" He knew it was Janie— the crowd's yelling must have drawn her to the bear pen. But he was too dizzy to see her face, and everything was starting to look blurry.

Just when he knew he could hang on no longer, he heard the bell. "Time!" yelled the bear-keeper. "Time!" He poked the bear with a long pole to distract her. Meanwhile a couple of strong farmers lunged forward and pulled Thomas from the back of the animal. Outside of the ring, Thomas' vision grew black.

When he came to, he was under a canopy, and a doctor was wrapping long strips of cloth around his ribs. Janie stood nearby, tears streaming down her cheeks. Edwin was there, too. And for once, his heartless cousin looked somewhat concerned. Thomas cringed inside when he saw that Grandfather was also in the tent.

The old man's face was a puzzle of emotions. But soon anger and disappointment seemed to take over. "How in the world could you do such a foolish thing?" Grandfather demanded. Thomas moaned, and slipped back into oblivion.

*   *   *

The deep gashes on his chest and neck healed very slowly. Each day the Rolfe's family physician came to Heacham Hall to tend them, and to check on Thomas' broken ribs. One day the doctor shook his head and said, "You will have the scars from those bear claws for the rest of your life."

For the rest of Thomas' break from college he continued to recover, but during this time Grandfather hardly spoke a word to him. His meals were sent to his room and he was never invited to join the family table. Thomas felt like Grandfather's disappointment was as painful as his injuries. And whenever Grandmother saw him, she looked upon him with tear-filled eyes. But Thomas knew that Grandfather had forbidden her to show any sympathy.

Finally in the first week of June, a messenger arrived from Cambridge to call Thomas back to college. The danger of epidemic was over, and only three students had died. Thomas was relieved to be able to return and to escape Grandfather's stony silence.

On his last evening at Heacham, he began to pack his things. He felt that he would *never* be forgiven for wrestling the bear. He had disgraced the entire family by acting like a common ruffian. They would be glad to see him go. Just as he fastened his bag, someone knocked on the door.

"Master Rolfe," called the maid. "Your grandfather has asked you to join him in the private sitting room of his bed chambers."

Thomas walked slowly to Grandfather's room. His heart felt like a lead weight in his chest. What could gandfather want? Perhaps he wanted to tell Thomas to leave this house and never come back. The door was open and Thomas quietly slipped inside, fearing the worst.

He found Grandfather in his chair, wrapped in heavy blankets. This seemed strange since the weather was warm. A candle burned on the big mahogany desk; its soft light reflected off the complete whiteness of Grandfather's hair. Suddenly Thomas felt horrible about angering this kind old man, who had taken such fine care of him over the years—raising him as if he were his own son. But as Thomas stood before him, he couldn't think of a single thing to say. He had already apologized, over and over.

Finally, Grandfather cleared his throat and spoke. "I received a very kind note from Miss Jane Poythress today."

Thomas blinked in surprise. "What did she say?"

"Well, she asked about your welfare of course. And then she mentioned something else—something that apparently was shared with her by your cousin Edwin, on the day of the Fair. Edwin informed Miss Poythress that you wrestled the bear because of a dare from his brother Jacob. And that by winning this dare you would also win ownership of the falcon, Lightning. Thomas, is this true?"

"Yes, sir, it is the truth." He dropped his head in shame.

Grandfather sighed. "I know how much that falcon means to you, Thomas. But it is right that I have punished you by showing you my anger. Your life is more important to us than anything! You cannot accept a challenge given to you by a fool, even if that fool is your own cousin. Have you learned this lesson?"

"Yes, sir, I believe that I have!" He sighed. It seemed that Grandfather had forgiven him at last! He hoped someday to thank Janie. How thoughtful she was to have written Grandfather an explanation for Thomas' foolishness! She had understood that Thomas' pride would not allow him to blame Jacob.

"And I must confess," continued Grandfather. "I will be very glad for the great falcon to be in your care."

Then he turned his chair toward his huge mahogany desk and unlocked a special drawer. He removed a heavy envelope and handed it to Thomas. The old envelope was still sealed with the crest of the Virginia Company stamped into the wax.

"I am almost seventy years old, my boy. And it seems I grow weaker each day. It is time we speak of things that are to come." His quivering voice was gentle with no more traces of anger.

"No, sir," Thomas injected. "You will live for many years." He didn't want to think about the possibility that Grandfather could die.

"Listen, lad. You are almost a man now. There are some things which I must explain to you."

Thomas grew silent and listened respectfully to the elderly Rolfe's speech.

"I wish that I had a large inheritance to give to you, Thomas. But the house and land of Heacham must go to your father's elder brother. I am glad that I have been able to pay for your education. You have a quick mind; perhaps that will take you further than any money I could have left you. And, of course, Moco, and now Lightning, will be left in your name."

"Thank you, Grandfather," Thomas spoke sincerely.

"But the future may hold more for you, Thomas. You know the lawyers of the Virginia Company in London received a copy of your father's will after he was slain. You are old enough now to have a copy of that will. I want you to read it now."

It was dated March 18, 1622. Only four days before Father's death, so he must have sensed that trouble was coming.... Thomas broke the seal on the envelope, and pulled out the top document. He began to read aloud.

> *The last Will and Testament of John Rolfe, from His Majesty's Colony in Virginia...Being of sound body, I do bequeath my home, the estate called Varina, and the land which I have claimed and all the soil which I have tilled and any crops which may be upon it, to my son Thomas Pepsicanough Rolfe, the child of my late wife, Lady Rebecca Pocahontas Rolfe. A copy of this estate is filed with the colony secretary in Jamestown.*

Attached to the will was a copy of another letter, one which John Rolfe had written earlier regarding the boundaries of his estate in 1617 when Mother was still alive.

> *...The goodness of this land will no doubt continue until the world's end. It is a country as worthy of high report as can be declared by the pen of the best writer. And we*

*living in Virginia are of all men on the earth most happy
and blessed.*

Thomas felt his eyes wet with tears. The loneliness he felt for
his father ached inside of him. Reading his father's wishes from
the will was like hearing his voice again.

"It wrenches my heart to read this, Grandfather," he said.
"But still, I do not plan to travel to Virginia and seek my fortunes
there. At one time, I would have gladly joined my father, but
since his murder, I have set my heart to remain in England. After
I finish school, I will seek my fortune here."

"I am glad for that, my boy," Grandfather answered. "You
know how your grandmother and I never wanted to see you
return to the perils of that savage land. But I knew that it was
right to entrust you with these communications. Now, Thomas,
look at the next document."

Thomas began to read the next legal paper. It was a message
to the factors of the Virginia Company in London from
Jamestown, dated 1624.

*The governor at Jamestown has received a communication
from Chief Opech in which Opech desires to see the son of
his niece, the Princess Pocahontas, the child Thomas Rolfe
who now lives in England. Opech states that he is willing
to give young Rolfe the lands left to him by Opech's brother
Powhatan. We colonists feel that this message is only an
attempt at further trickery on Opech's part, but still we feel
honor-bound to convey this message to the Rolfe family at
Heacham Hall.*

Thomas was shocked. To receive a message from the hated
wild man called Opech was beyond belief. He slammed his fist

onto Grandfather's solid desk. "It is a trick!" he cried. "A bloody rotten trick! Opech wishes he could kill me just like he killed my father!" Thomas ground his teeth in bitter unforgiveness.

"Yes, we all believe it is a trick. But you are old enough now that I felt I had to at least tell you of the message," Grandfather spoke solemnly. "Put the packet away for now, lad. I know it upsets you. Later, when you are back at college, you must read the other letter in the packet. It was written from your father to King James when he and your mother first came home to England. It will tell you much about your father's faith, and his spirit."

"I am afraid that I'm not a very spiritual person," Thomas said sadly.

"Yes, you are spiritual, Thomas," his grandfather replied. "God has created you that way. *Every* man is spirit, soul and body.

"Although I have remained a part of the Church of England, your father felt led to pursue the Puritan way. And your path may be different from either of us. But be confident of this one thing; many who love you have prayed for you, and I am confident that God will direct your spirit." Grandfather pushed away his blankets and rose to his feet. Thomas quickly came to his side.

"Now, lad, let me lean on your shoulder. You have been eating in your room alone for long enough. Let's get Grandmother, and we will all go down to dinner."

CHAPTER NINE

SPIRITUAL AWAKENING

THOMAS RETURNED TO CAMBRIDGE in June. He was quickly buried in his studies, working hard to make up for the two months that were lost to the scare of the Plague.

But the warm mid-summer days played havoc with his concentration. And finally one morning he could take it no longer. As he sat at his desk, daydreaming, he thought of Janie Poythress. Maybe he should write a letter to thank her for the note she had written to Grandfather. It was the first letter he'd ever written to a girl.

A few days later, the familiar envelope was back in his hands. His letter had been returned unopened. Janie must have changed her opinion of him that day at the Fair. She probably wanted nothing more to do with him, or surely she would have answered his letter. He tucked the note away and glanced out the window, but even the clear blue sky couldn't cheer him. Janie was the only girl he had ever felt close to.

"Thomas! Thomas Rolfe!" called someone from below his window. "It is the Sabbath! Close up those dusty books and come and join us!"

Thomas stuck his head out and peered down through the leaves of an ancient walnut tree. There below stood Professor Featherstone with a broad smile on his face.

"We're headed to a special service at the great church in Oxford. The famous Reverend Davenport is the most popular speaker in England. He is a great teacher—you'll like him. And we'll stop at the strawberry fields on the way."

"I'm coming!" Thomas called down. He bounded down the stairs, not thinking so much of a great speaker, but more about the promise of ripe strawberries! He needed a break from the books, and from his daydreaming about Janie. He ran and jumped on the back of Featherstone's wagon which was already loaded with a dozen of his friends.

As the wagon bumped along the boys began to sing. One loud ballad followed another. An older boy belted out a popular new song about Jamestown and Virginie. He then pounded Thomas on the back reminding him that he was a native of Virginia. Thomas smiled, it was all just good-natured fun. And Thomas didn't need to expose his real feelings about Jamestown.

The wagon drew nearer to the church and Thomas was astonished at the crowd that was gathered. Why such interest in a speaker in a college town? And yet men, women, and young people seemed to come to the church from all directions. Already the commons around the large building, and even the graveyard off to the side, were full!

Thomas slipped from the wagon, and pressed through the

crowd until he was close enough to see through a tall open window.

Reverend Davenport was already at the pulpit. "God created all men to have souls that are free!" The powerful words echoed through the ancient stonework. Thomas leaned forward and listened with intensity.

"Just this month I have been dismissed from my pastorate of St. Stephen's in London," Davenport announced. The crowd gasped. Thomas had learned on the wagon ride that Reverend Davenport was the most famous pastor of their time! How could the Bishop recently appointed by the new King Charles, take such an action against this popular man of God?

"But still I will not lose courage. I will remain free before God in my actions. Free in my speaking and preaching," the minister concluded. "Free in my actions! Free in my spirit!"

The crowd began to cheer. And it was the student, and his own friends who cheered the loudest. Thomas found himself cheering with them. Reverend Davenport's words on freedom seemed to pierce his heart. Professor Featherstone had been right about this man!

Later, Reverend Samuel Hooker spoke. He was followed by a handsome young man named John Eliot, who had graduated from Jesus College just a few years before. Eliot spoke of the disciples and other characters from the Bible as if they were real men. People that Thomas might actually meet and speak to.

Thomas became lost in the great stories. As he listened to Eliot, the Gospels became alive to him for the first time.

Finally it was time for the Cambridge students to pile back into the wagon. The next stop would be the strawberry fields. But suddenly strawberries were nothing compared to the questions that tumbled through Thomas' mind. He hurried to sit beside his teacher.

"Mr. Featherstone, are these speakers Puritans like my father was?" he asked.

"Not really. They are called Congregationalists. They haven't broken away from the Church of England, like the Puritans. They simply believe that each congregation and pastor should not be controlled by the King's Bishop in London."

Congregationalists. That was a new word for Thomas.

Soon Featherstone stopped the wagon and the boys jumped down and raced to the summer treat that was free for the taking. Thomas stuffed himself at the berry field, and even filled his hat with the big ripe strawberries to carry back to the dorm. Then it was time for the wagon to head back to Cambridge.

Just as the wagon reached College bridge, two armed guards stepped forward and blocked their way. Thomas and the others looked on with interest. They had never had reason to fear a royal guard.

"Have you been to Davenport's meeting in Oxford?" one of the guards loudly demanded. "If so, each of you owes the royal treasury one schilling."

"But this was not a Puritan meeting! We were listening to men from the Church of England," protested Featherstone. "How dare you make us pay this fine!"

"It doesn't matter, this meeting was not sanctioned by His Lordship the Bishop of England. Davenport, Hooker, and Eliot are rebellious men. And any who attended their meeting will also be fined. Now pay up, one and all."

Featherstone and all of the students were shocked, but each one dug into their pockets and paid the fine. Everyone grumbled, but Thomas was furious. This was more than just a bothersome tax. This new decree was wrong!

Back in his room, he stared at his school books without even seeing them. His mind was filled with the stirring words he had heard from the great teachers. It looked as if many more fines would have to come out of his poor student pockets. He knew he could not stay away from these men who had somehow made Faith come alive for him.

The next morning Thomas grabbed his pile of books and papers and headed to his Monday class. But when he rushed through the Quadrant, he noticed the boys all around him were whispering and chattering.

"What's happened?" he asked his friend Andrew. "Another threat of the Plague?"

"No," said Andrew in hushed tones. "But a lot of students *are* missing for another reason today. A notice was posted that any student with a Puritan father, or with Puritan leanings, has been banned from college by an edict of the Bishop in London. Timmons is gone, as well as Joseph Adams and Will Richards."

Will Richards! Thomas was shocked. *Will had been banned from the school because of this new law.* School would not be the same without Will. He had been Thomas' friend since the first day in Cambridge. He was a great rower, and a great wrestling opponent. Now he was forced away from his education, just because his father had taken the Puritan Oath. Thomas wondered if he might be next—after all even though his father was dead, he had been a Puritan.

He walked slowly to class. He was not a Puritan like his father had been. Yet he was not an Anglican like his grandparents, either. But he did feel drawn to the road between the two. Maybe he was a Congregationalist. And maybe, like Grandfather had promised, God was leading him on his own spiritual way.

Thomas remembered something that Captain John Smith had told him long ago. Back in the Chesapeake, every Algonquin man on a spiritual quest made a secret path through the forest. Each one was different. Was this what Thomas was experiencing, a spiritual quest? "God," he whispered, "help me find my own path."

*　　*　　*

March 2, 1629

"Hear ye! Hear ye! Parliament has been dissolved. By the actions of King Charles, Parliament has been dissolved!" Shouts of the Town Crier rang throughout the Cambridge square. Thomas pressed through the crowd to grab one of the leaflets. It was true! King Charles had dismissed the legal government of all of Britain!

Someone in the crowd yelled, "Down with the King! Down with the Bishop! Down with the Anglican Church!" The voice was quickly joined by others.

But then another group began shouting, "No! Down with those cursed Puritans! They have caused this!"

For almost a year now, Thomas had attended the Congregationalist meetings. And for almost a year, the preachers had warned that something like this might happen. There was even talk of a civil war!

Thomas' mind reeled as he walked to the stable where he now boarded Moco and grandfather's prized falcons. Grandfather Rolfe had died last winter. And since then, Thomas had found comfort in keeping the horse and falcons nearby. Now he saddled Moco and headed toward the little village of Chelmsford.

He would visit his friend, John Eliot. Thomas had spent many a Sunday listening to this wise young minister. If anyone could understand what was happening, it would be his good friend John.

"Hello there! John!" Thomas called as he reined Moco to a stop in from of the thatched-roof cottage.

"I'm glad you've come!" said John. He warmly shook Thomas' hand and pulled him inside. "This is a dark day for us all."

John Eliot was more than ten years older than Thomas, but his brilliance and energy had caused Thomas to look to him as a friend and as a hero. In the past, Thomas had often felt that others, like his cousins, were jealous of him because of his strength and his mind. But John Eliot had the confidence that came from true character. He always encouraged Thomas. He always made Thomas feel that he could be great, and do great things.

"What does Reverend Hooker think of this news?" asked Thomas. Reverend Hooker was the Senior Pastor and mentor to all the Congregationalists.

"Reverend Hooker is gone," confided John. "The King's men put a price on his head. Last night we disguised him, and he has fled to Holland."

"But the Reverend is not a rebel!" Thomas couldn't imagine that things could be so bad.

"No, but he speaks his mind and preaches what he believes God would have him say. That's enough to make him a marked man. I've remained behind to find a ship to take his wife Susanna and myself to the New World. We hope Reverend Hooker will soon join us there."

"Then you're leaving, too? You're going to the Colonies?" Thomas gasped. How could this be happening? How could he lose his dear friend, John Eliot?

"Yes, I'm headed to the place called Massachusetts Bay. You have often heard us speak of this possibility."

"I know," Thomas groaned. "But I didn't think you would really leave."

"Dozens of us plan to go. Many from this village alone. We can no longer stay where we cannot worship with freedom."

John unfurled a long blue silk banner which was laying on the table. It was embroidered with the new Seal of Massachusetts. "Look, this is our banner!" Eliot said proudly. "It was designed by the Earl of Lincoln and his sister, the Lady Arabella." Thomas' mouth dropped open when he saw the image on the banner. It was an Algonquin Indian, and words from the Bible: *Come over and help us.*

"Thomas, why don't you join us in the New World?" John placed a hand on his shoulder. "Massachusetts is pretty close to Jamestown!"

"No." Thomas tried to swallow the lump growing in his throat. "You don't know the dangers of that savage land."

"We are in great danger here, my friend," John answered seriously.

*   *   *

Several weeks later, Thomas rode Moco from Cambridge to Oxford. As he traveled, Thomas thought of his friends Reverend Hooker and John Eliot. They were far out on the sea by now. On their way to America. He missed them terribly. And with Grandfather gone he felt isolated and alone. Who could he turn to for counsel now? The whole stable world of England had turned upside down.

Thomas reached Oxford and his destination, the famous Bodlean Library. Captain John Smith had written Thomas about something very special that had recently been deeded to this library.

Thomas spoke quietly to the uniformed trustee. "I am Thomas Pepsicanough Rolfe, the son of John Rolfe and Princess Pocahontas. I have come to see the great mantle of Chief Powhatan, my grandfather."

"Come with me, Master Rolfe," the trustee said kindly. He led Thomas to an elaborate cabinet, and opened the door. It was the first time Thomas had actually seen the mantle. He didn't know what to say, and was glad when the trustee left him alone with the treasure.

He reached out and grasped the long, heavy cloak with both hands. As he fingered the soft garment he remembered the story his mother told him. Long ago, King James had sent Grandfather Powhatan a long royal robe and crown, as well as the kingly gift of a greyhound dog. Grandfather Powhatan had then taken his cape from his own shoulders, and sent it back to England to King James.

Thomas ran his fingers carefully over the hundreds of tiny white shells that had been sewn into a beautiful pattern of a man surrounded by mighty stags. He knew his mother, the Princess Pocahontas, had sewn on many of these shells with her own hands.

As Thomas touched Grandfather Powhatan's cape, the people of the Chesapeake forest seemed strangely close to him. Almost as if he could see and hear them—in his heart—and he remembered the words that were sewn on the Massachusetts banner, beneath the picture of the Algonquin: *Come over and help us.* Tears filled his eyes.

And as he rode Moco back to Cambridge, *Come over and help us* echoed through his mind again and again.

*   *   *

The next morning, Thomas awoke and dressed quickly. He ran across the common area. History was his favorite class, and he was eager to share with Professor Featherstone what it was like to see Powhatan's robe.

Thomas pushed open the door, but the students in the classroom were in an uproar. And Professor Featherstone was nowhere to be seen.

"Thomas, a horrible thing has happened, a devilish thing!" one of his friends exclaimed. "Professor Featherstone's father owns the ship that took John Eliot and Mrs. Hooker and some others to the New World. Last night the Professor was taken away by the Bishop's guards and questioned about his friends and about his faith."

Another student interrupted, "They beat the Professor! And, worse yet, they have marked him for life! They have cut off the Professor's ears!"

Thomas slumped into a chair. Professor Featherstone beaten? His ears cut off? Treated like a common thief or criminal? What had England become?

If good, decent men like Professor Featherstone could be treated like this, then England could no longer be a place to call home.

*   *   *

Six days later, Thomas stood upon the bustling wharf in the sea town of Bristol. His skin tingled with excitement in the cold ocean breeze. He breathed in the pungent smells of salt and fish and tar. For the first time in ages he felt totally alive. He admired the ships clustered in the harbor, with their tall masts and wide spars. The largest ship at the dock was the *Lyon,* to be captained by old Commander Featherstone, Professor Featherstone's father.

Thomas had sold Moco to Uncle Edward in order to gain money for passage. He had been worried that his powerful horse would be injured in the roughness of a sea journey. But after he stroked Moco's coat for one last time, tears had streamed down his face. He knew he would never see Moco or Heacham again.

Now Thomas turned his face to the sea. There was no turning back now. On his arm, proud and fierce in her silver hood, perched the falcon, Lightning. The handsome bird caused men and women on the dock to turn and stare with interest and amusement.

"Do you find the name of Thomas Rolfe on your list?" he asked the seaman who blocked the gangplank of the *Lyon.* The bearded man sternly checked names off a long scroll.

"Yes, indeed," he bellowed after only a short pause. "Captain Featherstone has found room for ye! Any friend of his son is a friend of the captain's!"

"And...how about my falcon?" Thomas said with concern. "I cannot sail without her."

The big Irishman laughed with a good-natured rumble. "Yes, indeed. The captain said there would be room on his ship for a fine hunting falcon such as yours!"

Soon the anchor was weighed, and the great sails unfurled and snapped in the wind. The crowd on the shore cheered and waved, and church bells rang from the towers. The tall ship slipped gracefully down the channel. In a few hours, Thomas saw brightly colored houses on the southern shore of Wales. But before long, all traces of land were out of sight. Thomas looked westward as they pushed through rolling waters, and the dangers of the open sea.

CHAPTER TEN

THE CHESAPEAKE

IT HAD BEEN A GOOD CROSSING, but after ten weeks at sea, Thomas' eyes grew hungry for land. Captain Featherstone said they were fortunate; they had only one real storm, and plenty of strong westerly winds to propel the ship. But just the same, the passengers on the crowded boat were growing restless.

Thomas was restless too. He paced the decks like a caged tiger. It was already June; how he longed to see green fields and trees. Finally he stopped by the wooden perch the captain had set up for Lightning. He untied the cord from the great bird's leg and removed the hood. Then Thomas raised his arm in the hunt signal, and Lightning soared to the sky. A small crowd of children gathered at the ship's railing with wide eyes and hushed whispers.

Thomas only freed her on days like today when the weather was good, and the wind and waves were not too strong. Within seconds, Lightning flew in wide circles around the ship. Thomas could tell her keen eyes were studying the silvery shadows in the waves below. Now many of the older passengers gathered as well—watching Lightning fly was a highlight of their day.

The crowd watched as the bird dove, plunging like an arrow toward the sea. She brushed the top of the salt water, then snatched a fish from its surface. The fish wiggled in her claws as Lightning circled the ship once again, showing off her prize. Then she swooped low and dropped the fish right onto the deck.

The children ran forward, pushing to see who could grab the flopping fish. Thomas laughed out loud with the mothers and fathers who watched this contest. "Lightning has given us the greatest moments on this voyage!" boomed Captain Feather-stone. He stood by Thomas to watch the still-circling bird.

Then Lightning headed back into the heavens. She began to circle farther and farther away. She had never gone so far from the ship before. Finally she became a tiny speck on the horizon, moving in uneven dips and dives.

Thomas grew worried. What if she lost the ship? What if she never returned? At last the dot grew bigger, and he saw Lightning winging her way closer. Once again, she held something in her talons. For a moment, Thomas thought it might be a seagull; they had seen some lately. But, no, it was a plump goose! The kind of goose that only flew close to land!

And in that same instant, the ship's bell began to clang furiously, and a sailor high in the crow's nest yelled, "Land Ho! Virginie straight ahead!"

Thomas climbed one of the long ropes up the rigging, and peered toward the land of his birth. There ahead lay the land of Pocahontas. The land of the Algonquin.

They sailed into the waters of the wide Chesapeake and on into the mouth of the slow-moving James River. The low hills on both sides were densely wooded, fronted by marshy grasslands and sandy beaches. Lazy cranes flew along the top of the water, and the ship plowed its way through hundreds of ducks and honking geese. After ten weeks at sea, it looked like paradise!

They passed a bend in the river and Thomas sighted what he knew must be Jamestown! A triangular fort sat huddled on a small peninsula, and over the wooden walls, he spotted a steeple and some colorful flags.

He was amazed at the number of homes that stretched beyond the walls of the fort, and disappeared up into the tall timber in the distance. It was incredible! Despite ambush and disease, there must be over a thousand people in the colony now! And at least a hundred were gathered to cheer the ship's arrival.

Thomas ran down the gangplank just as it was being lowered. He pushed through the crowd gathered on the dock, and rushed toward land. The scent in the air and the feel of the breeze stirred childhood memories. When his boots touched the ground, he fell to his knees.

"I have come home, Mother," he whispered out loud. He leaned over and scooped up two handfuls of sandy earth and held them to his chest. Whatever might lay ahead, this would be his *home*. Forever. He slowly rose to his feet and let out a big sigh. He felt a peace inside him that hadn't been there since his mother's death.

The sound of voices drew his attention to the water's edge. A group of natives gathered there were bartering over items laid out upon the beach. He could not tell if they were Chicka-homonies, or Potomacs, or his own Powhatan clan. But the language they spoke was the soft, melodious Algonquian. And a few words were familiar echoes in his memory. He set his mind to relearn that language, right away.

They were the first Chesapeake natives he had seen since childhood. He admired how their straight black hair and copper skin shown in the sunlight. Most of the men wore deerskin loincloths. But some wore European coats, and others had rich fur capes. Their knee-high moccasins were fringed and decorated with shells and beads. The men were tall and strong. Just like him.

He walked a little closer, but not so close as to draw attention to himself. They had brought a variety of items to barter—wild turkeys, lobsters, mussels and clams, thick beaver and fox pelts, and carved wooden bowls. They bargained for pieces of iron, copper kettles, tools and cloth. Some paid with blue-black shells strung on leather strips. Thomas remembered this was called *wampum.*

After they packed up to leave, the Algonquins stepped into slender wooden canoes. Thomas was surprised at how they sped through the water with quiet smoothness. These graceful canoes looked far faster than the best skiffs he had rowed in England. How he'd love to get his hands on one! Finally when the last of the canoes pulled away from the shore, he decided it was time to explore the rough city called Jamestown.

He walked through the tall fort gates and over to the long log building that flew the colorful flags. In front of the building stood a dozen uniformed soldiers. But the doors of the building were open wide, and Thomas saw that he was free to enter. Behind a rough wooden counter stood an official with a ruddy, weather-beaten face.

"Good day to you, sir," said Thomas. "I am Thomas Rolfe. I have come to ask about my legal claim to the land of my late father, John Rolfe."

"Well, bless my soul!" the man exclaimed with a huge smile. "The son of good John Rolfe. Then you are the son of Poca-hontas!"

"Yes, sir, I am."

Another man in uniform rose from a desk in the corner and came forward to clasp Thomas' hand. "I am so glad to see you again, Thomas. So very glad to see you!" said the big man.

Thomas searched the officer's eyes for some trace of mem-ory. At last it hit him. "Colonel Poythress!" he exclaimed. This was Janie's father!

"I am in charge of military matters here in Jamestown now, and I am delighted to welcome you to our post. I remember our trip to your Scottish hunting lodge with great fondness."

"Thank you, sir!" How good it was to see a familiar face. "I have come here to reopen my father's claim on Varina. But I also need directions so I can get there."

"The legal claim is no problem," the colonel assured him. "Providing you're willing to restore the military blockhouse on your land. We require this for all outpost property. But I must warn you, after all this time, the land and what's left of the house is probably in a bad state." Thomas' heart sank a little. He hadn't considered that the place might not be habitable.

The colonel smiled. "Besides that, after your long journey, you should stay in the fort with us for a few days, Thomas. Then I can ride out to Varina with you myself."

"That would be nice, if it's no trouble," said Thomas. He knew that was wise, but his heart still longed to go to Varina.

"Of course it's no trouble. And this way you can attend our service of Thanksgiving. We have one whenever a ship arrives. And tonight, there's a welcoming dance with fiddle music and fine spiced cider. You can't miss it! Besides, I know someone who just might like to see you!" said the colonel with a twinkle in his eye. "Just over a year ago, I brought my family over to join me. Weren't you and Jane good friends when you were little?"

"Why, yes, sir. I remember her. I remember her well." So this was why his letter had been returned to him unopened last term. She had already departed for the Chesapeake.

The colonel showed Thomas to the military barracks. There he found a place to bathe and rest. Just as he put the final polish on his boots, he heard the happy sound of fiddle music calling the townspeople to the fort's commons. Thomas entered the celebration and was instantly greeted by several men. He lost track of their names as they pounded him on the back and shook his hand.

"Your father was a good friend of mine," said a small thin man. "John Rolfe was a truly great man," said a man not much older than Thomas.

One burly man told Thomas how he had survived the massacre of 1622. "My name is Samuel Gookin and my plantation is beyond Varina a ways, so I'm your neighbor. When I come to town for supplies, I'll be sure to stop by. And if you want to see *real* wilderness," he winked, "come on out to my place."

Thomas thanked him and moved toward the middle of the town square where a grand bonfire crackled and snapped. A fiddler in a highland kilt played a happy tune, and couples danced a country reel around the fire. Thomas noticed with surprise that there were quite a number of young women in the crowd. But then he remembered a story he'd heard about a ship that had brought a boatload of brides to Virginia not long ago.

He was attempting to blend with the group and quietly

observe his new friends and neighbors, when he noticed a slender figure in a flowing silken dress moving toward him. She extended her hand in greeting, and smiled up at him with a pretty face and big blue eyes, framed by a mound of soft, reddish curls.

"Hello, Thomas Pepsicanough." Her words were soft, but her smile was big and genuine.

"Jane! Jane Poythress!" he stammered as he looked down at her. "I was glad to learn from your father that you had come to Jamestown. I remember you told me this was your dream—many years ago."

Jane laughed. "Yes, and I remember that was the day you knocked me off my horse!"

"I was trying to save you!" protested Thomas. And they both laughed. Suddenly Thomas felt completely at ease. "Miss Poythress," he bowed slightly. "Can you trust me enough to join me in a dance? I know I missed an opportunity to dance the maypole with you once, but I think I can manage a country reel!"

"Yes, Pepsi!" She took his outstretched arm. "I would be happy to dance with you."

The next morning, Thomas worshiped at the service of Thanksgiving. He sat beside Colonel Poythress and the other men on the right side of the church. All of the women sat on the left. In this New World church there were Anglicans, Puritans, and Congregationalists—all joined together. A ripple of pride ran through him when he thought how this church stood on the same site as the chapel where his parents had been wed. He prayed God would allow his parents to see he was here, praising God in the Chesapeake, just as they had done.

After a Scotsman ended the service with a moving hymn on a bagpipe, Thomas turned to the colonel. "I must go on to Varina tomorrow," he said firmly. "My heart won't let me wait any longer."

The colonel nodded. "All right, young man. I'll be ready to join you at sunrise. Mr. Gookin's barge will bring your trunks and supplies up the river, while we go on ahead. And I have given Jane permission to accompany us—she is anxious for a chance to be away from the fort."

"Will it be safe for her to go with us?"

"Well, now and then we deal with some unexpected treachery from renegades. But since the massacre, the military has made such fierce reprisals, the majority of the tribesmen are in check. And my Jane is good with her pistol, and in danger she's as fast a rider as ever you could find."

"Yes, sir, I believe that," Thomas nodded.

Early the next morning, Thomas mounted the huge horse he had purchased at the dock. Her name was Brandy, and though she wasn't as swift as Moco, her strength would be useful for both plowing and riding. Jane and her father joined him and they rode out of Jamestown and turned to the north. North toward Varina. The colonel had told him it was a thirty-mile ride.

As they rode, the colonel described the lay of the land, and although Thomas listened intently, he stole occasional glances at Jane. Today she wore a dark woolen riding skirt and sat sidesaddle, the way a proper lady should. But her excited cheerfulness reminded him of when she was still a girl. Her personality was warm like the sunshine on the golden fields around them, and Thomas was very glad she had come.

He felt natural and relaxed with Jane. The quietness he normally felt around girls back at Cambridge disappeared. He asked her the names of plants and trees as they passed, and she told him both the English names and the Indian names. She also told him about the families whose farms they rode by. Many had endured great hardships.

"The Chesapeake has not been easy on my family," she said. "Father and Mother have both suffered with the shaking sickness, and my little brother drowned in the freezing river soon after we came. I miss him a lot.... But I still have my two sisters. And Virginia is our home. I love it more each day!"

As they traveled, Thomas told them more about his life. He also updated them about the growing strife in England. He even talked about his plans for the future.

"I have great dreams for Varina. I have all of my father's letters, and I find I'm already experiencing his love for this land. I hope someday to meet some of my mother's relatives. I even brought over the Bible that King James had promised to her. Before he died he asked me to bring it to the Algonquin."

"That's wonderful!" exclaimed Jane. "And will you?"

Thomas paused. "Of course I want it to get to my mother's people, but I will never, never accept my Uncle Opech's invitation to come to Werowocomoco. I could never look upon his face without wanting to kill him. But I know my revenge would only bring harm to both Algonquin and English alike."

At the mention of Opech's name, Colonel Poythress spat on the ground. Thomas knew the colonel had come to Jamestown right after the Massacre of '22, and that he had helped set hundreds of markers on the colonists' unmarked graves.

By afternoon, the three riders came over a hill and trotted

through wide, fertile meadows. "We are on your land now!" the colonel shouted. They passed the abandoned lookout tower with its simple blockade wall. The one that Thomas had promised to restore.

Suddenly he could wait no longer. He urged his horse to a gallop and thundered down to the river. He knew from his father's letters that the homesite was down there. He reached a clearing with a beautiful view of the water. Centered in the lush green overgrown grass were the ruins of a once-lovely house. A place his parents had called home.

Thomas dismounted and walked through the rubble. Jane and the colonel did not join him, and for this he was thankful. He needed a moment to gather his thoughts and take in what had once been his parents' dream.

The roof was caved in, leaving the upstairs almost useless. The downstairs was partially burned, and wild vines from the field had climbed in through the doorway and windows. Some intrusive vines had even swallowed up broken bits of furniture. Some furnishings were still intact—an old oak table, a few scarred chairs. But for the most part, it looked completely hopeless.

The fields were even worse. The weeds and trees of the forest had returned with incredible speed. He walked down by the river, and all that remained of his father's wharf were a few old timber piers sticking up from the river bottom.

He heard quiet footsteps brushing through the grass behind him. He jerked around, not knowing what to expect. An ambush perhaps? But it was Jane. She joined him, and together they stood in silence and surveyed Varina's ruins. He turned and saw that Jane's eyes were full of understanding.

Then she grabbed his hand and pulled him over to the old well. She began to crank a rusty iron handle, but it was too hard, and he reached over to help. Before long an old bucket rose. It was overflowing with water!

"Look, Pepsi, your well is still full!" exclaimed Jane. "This is a sign of good fortune!" He dipped his cupped hands into the water. It was fresh and clean! He splashed it on his face, and felt his courage return.

It would take courage, and a lot more, to remake something of this forlorn homestead. And all around him lay the Chesa-peake—a wild and dangerous and untamed country. His destiny, as the son of the Princess Pocahontas and the Puritan John Rolfe, had placed him right in the middle of it.

CHAPTER ELEVEN

THE WARRIOR

A FEW WEEKS LATER, Thomas stood at the top of the rickety wooden look-out on the edge of his land. He had begun to restore and maintain the outpost as promised. But the high log fence still had some gaping holes. Today he worked on the two-story tower. There were slits cut into the walls so that a man could see and defend himself against attackers.

He shoved his shoulder against a fallen timber and pushed it back into place. He then pounded a large nail into the wooden wall. He was thankful for the heavy hammer he had purchased back in Bristol. All his tools were like gold to him now.

As he worked, a shadow regularly passed across the tower. On most mornings, he allowed Lightning to fly free, and seek her own food. And the strong hunter often returned with a plump squirrel for him. He knew that as much as she loved to fly freely around the lands of Varina, she would always return when he whistled.

Thomas pounded in another big nail. The sound of his hammer echoed in the quietness of the meadow. Suddenly, Lightning screamed a warning. His arm froze in mid-swing and he turned to look. Someone was approaching. He instinctively reached for his gun, but before he raised it, he heard a voice call his name in the distance. It was Jane! She rode into the clearing, the colonel close behind her. As they drew near he could see they were loaded down, and he ran down to meet them.

"Good day, Thomas," called Jane. "It looks like you're making good progress."

"Come see," he called back and pointed over to the house. In just a few weeks, he had worked hard to make the house more livable. He knew that when winter came, it would be hard. He proudly showed Jane and the colonel all he had done. No glass was available to restore his windows, so he had covered them with thick oil paper. He had even made a few pieces of furniture, and his good neighbor, Mr. Gookin, had brought bricks over to rebuild the fireplace.

"You've done a wonderful job!" exclaimed Jane as they stood in his keeping room. She handed him a bundle of what looked like quilts and rugs. "And these are to make it more cozy, and hopefully help keep you warm in the winter."

The colonel laid some more provisions on the table. "Mrs. Poythress thought you might be able to use some herbs and spices and things to make cooking a little more interesting for you. The winter can be long, and game meat will all start to taste the same after awhile."

"Thank you," said Thomas, touched by their kindness. He carried the quilts over to his large wooden trunk to store until the weather grew colder. When he opened the lid, he lifted out the special King James Bible. "This is the Bible I told you about."

The colonel walked over and took the large book into his hands with admiration. "This is a real treasure, Thomas."

Thomas reached into the trunk again and pulled out the tiny carved case that held the precious pearl necklace and earrings. He opened it and showed it to Jane. "These were a gift to my mother from her father, Powhatan."

"These are beautiful," breathed Jane. She touched the pearls with one finger, as if afraid to hurt them.

"This necklace and the earrings will belong to my wife one day," he said quietly without looking up. When he closed the case, he noticed a blush across Janie's cheek.

"Those are valuable, son," said the colonel. He handed the Bible back to him. "I hope you keep these treasures in a safe place. Now, Janie dear, I think we need to start back, in order to make the fort before dark."

"Thank you again," called Thomas as the two rode away.

It was late in the afternoon, but he headed back over to the army blockhouse. There was still much work to be done. Before dusk, he had one wall completely repaired. He stepped back to stretch and admire his work.

Suddenly, a fierce scream from Lightning pierced the cool evening air. Thomas knew the bird's eyes were like a pirate's scope, and she was the best warning system in the colony. He dropped his hammer and grabbed up his rifle. Two sets of visitors in one day seemed unlikely! And this time, no one called out a greeting.

He saw nothing from the blockhouse, but Lightning continued to screech. Thomas jumped down from the building and ran over to the tall timber which had been left like a ship's mast inside the walls of the outpost. The tree's seventy-foot height was set in climbing cleats like a ladder, and at the top was a large iron pot containing dry firewood that could be lit as a warning if an enemy was sighted.

He scurried to the top of the timber just in time to see a powerful-looking Algonquin man slip away from the clearing and back into the forest. Thomas was shaken. He had sensed he was being watched lately, but thought it might be his imagination due to the unaccustomed loneliness. And now this proved it! But who could this Algonquin warrior be? What if he was a spy sent from Opech?

Night was coming, so Thomas whistled for Lightning and returned to his house. But the worry still nagged him as he roasted a joint of meat for his dinner. That night he awoke in a cold sweat, with the remnants of a nightmare running through his mind. He had dreamed that he was single-handedly fighting off dozens of fierce warriors to protect his father; but when the warriors had run off, his father was already dead.

The next morning he woke up determined to put these fears and concerns behind him. He needed a break from all this hard work. He decided it was a good time to try his hand at fishing.

He had seen the shadows of huge fish beneath the muddy river water. And Mr. Gookin had told him that now was the best time to catch the big ones! He already had plenty of flour and beans to last the winter, and with Lightning's squirrels, and any luck in fishing, he might just make it until next summer's harvest. Next year, he would plant a cash crop, and raise enough produce to make it easily through the following winter.

He grabbed up his heavy fishing rod. It had landed him a big salmon just last year in England. He also took his long-handled Scottish net, the best that money could buy. At the end of a strong line, he tied his biggest hook, and then waded deep into the cold, swirling river water. With a long swing of the pole, he threw the line out into the middle.

In that very same instant, he felt a mighty jerk on the pole. Already a fish had hit the hook! Thomas quickly pulled on the line, then gasped at the enormous size of the fish as it flipped on top of the water. It must be over eight feet long! Its scales looked like a serpent's! Before he could think, the monster fish jerked him under the water. Thomas struggled to his feet as the huge snake-like fish swam around him. Common sense suggested that he release the huge fish, but he couldn't bear to let this one get away! He struggled to get his salmon net placed just right in front of the fish. But the serpent-fish cut through the net like it was made of cobwebs!

Then, with a mighty flail of its eight-foot length, the monster knocked Thomas beneath the water again. This time his head slammed against a boulder as he went down, and then everything went black.

The next thing he knew, a force was tugging on the back of his shirt and something pulled him from the water and dropped him on the bank. Thomas opened his eyes just in time to see a huge, powerful man stab the flailing monster-fish with a mighty spear! The man was stripped to the waist and his muscles bulged with determined force. It was the same Algonquin warrior he had spotted yesterday!

The strong native glanced over at Thomas, then turned back to the huge fish that was pinned in the mud by his long spear. Thomas sat on the bank, sputtering and gasping for breath as he witnessed the man smack the serpent on the head with a large stone club, then pull the long limp body from the water. Thomas wondered if he would be next. He pulled up his legs, ready to run.

"Pepsicanough," called the man. "You die this way! You do

not know how to fish for the mighty sturgeon. I must teach you."

Thomas looked at the stranger in complete amazement. Then the Algonquin leaned down to the river and retrieved what remained of the Scottish salmon net. When he saw how it was shredded, he laughed out loud. Then he raised his arm in greeting.

"I am Parahunt," the handsome warrior announced. "Son of Powhatan, Brother of Pocahontas."

So it was Parahunt that Thomas had observed slipping into the forest yesterday! Thomas invited him into his house.

"I have come often to watch over my favorite sister's son. I stayed out of sight, because I did not know if I would be welcome," explained Parahunt as Thomas hung his shirt to dry near the fire.

"You are most welcome here!" declared Thomas. "You will always be welcome."

Parahunt told him that he was the chief of his own village. Thomas felt deeply moved that Chief Parahunt would make personal visits to Varina.

"I was given something which once belonged to you!" Thomas exclaimed. From its pouch hanging next to the fireplace, he proudly removed the tomahawk, given to him long ago by Captain John Smith.

Parahunt held the tomahawk. "Ahh, John Smith Nantaquod. He did well to give you my tomahawk. And did my old friend teach you how to throw it, as I taught him?"

"Well, he tried…" Thomas tried not to remember the chicken.

"Parahunt shall teach you better," said his uncle, with a wide grin.

In the next few weeks, Parahunt often showed up unexpectedly. He patiently taught Thomas how to throw the tomahawk, and how to spear and club the mighty sturgeon. But this, he explained, was only the beginning.

Parahunt brought corn, squash, and dried berries from his own village storehouse. He showed Thomas how to set traps and snares that could catch beaver, rabbits, raccoons and wild turkeys. He even introduced Thomas to popcorn.

He showed Thomas how to catch fish at night by holding a torch from a canoe to attract them. And Parahunt gave Thomas a strong bow and sharp arrows, and he showed him how to practice. Thomas had been a good marksman with the English cross-bow and he quickly mastered this lightweight, more accurate weapon.

Whenever he came to Varina, Parahunt was always amazed and impressed with Thomas' great falcon, Lightning. Each time the bird swooped home with prey in her claws, the warrior whooped with wonder. He had never seen anything equal to this.

"Your hunting bird is a great Manitou! She is mighty like an eagle, yet she comes to your arm. This is a powerful sign, Pepsicanough," Parahunt spoke gravely. "A powerful sign."

Now when Parahunt used Thomas' Algonquin name, it seemed the most natural thing in the world. And whenever he was with his uncle, Thomas practiced his native language. It came easily to him, like a hazy dream being slowly remembered.

But more than just learning Algonquin customs, Thomas found he was actually learning the Algonquin way of thinking, the Algonquin way of being. As he followed Parahunt's example, his body became as tough as iron. He had always been strong, but now he became lean, and his endurance was strengthened.

"My own little boys had to practice shooting every morning," Parahunt told him. "They were not allowed a bite of food until they hit their marks. Our weapons are not as strong as guns, but we never run out of powder or ammunition." Thomas knew that Parahunt's sons were grown men now, and two of them lived far to the north and ruled their own small villages.

Often Parahunt would run and work a whole day without stopping to eat, and Thomas Pepsi worked hard to keep up. It was amazing—Parahunt was more than twice his age, but he was still an awesome warrior.

*   *   *

Several months had passed since Pepsi had met his uncle. Parahunt had shown him how to tend the squash and corn that were growing wild, and now his fields looked fine and healthy. One steamy, sticky day in late summer, Pepsi grabbed up his fishing spear and headed for the river.

Just as he reached the water's edge, he spotted Parahunt paddling toward him in a sleek canoe. "Hello, nephew," called Parahunt. "You have bragged about the way you won races on the rivers of England. It is time you came out onto the water with me to show me how well you do with an Algonquin canoe!"

Pepsi was pleased with the challenge. He tossed his cotton shirt and boots up high on the bank and splashed out into the water, then carefully climbed into the slender boat. Parahunt handed him a paddle and sat back, arms crossed upon his chest. Pepsi began to row, determined to master the Algonquin craft.

He quickly found that this kind of rowing was far different

from the double oars of the Cambridge college boats. At first, his strokes were unsure. But he kept at it, learning to appreciate the way the canoe was built; light as a feather, but able to shoot through the water when handled right. Soon he mastered the strokes and paddled like a warrior. Parahunt nodded his approval. Pepsi paused on the other side of the wide James River. He pulled in his oar and wiped his brow.

"Too hot," Parahunt grunted. "Let's swim." And before Pepsi could say a word, Parahunt tipped the canoe sideways and slid into the water.

Pepsi was caught off-balance when the canoe tipped so quickly, and he, too, fell into the water. He began to dog-paddle. It was the only stroke he knew. "You swim like a clumsy white man for sure!" Parahunt laughed good-naturedly as he glided through the water like a fish. "Come on over here, and I will show you the Algonquin way to breathe under the water."

Parahunt was in an area where tall reeds grew at the river's edge. Pepsi watched as Parahunt broke off a long piece of reed, and held it out so he could see the reed was hollow. He then placed one end of the reed in his mouth, lay back, and stretched out on the bottom of the river. The other end of the reed still stuck out of the water. Pepsi realized his uncle had made a breathing tube!

Pepsi quickly broke off his own reed and tried it. He too sank to the bottom of the river and lay on his back. He was surprised at how easy it was to breathe through the long reed. He even opened his eyes and looked about. Parahunt lay under the water only a few feet away. They both remained perfectly still. Soon, a small school of fish swam by, followed by a long eel. This was truly wonderful!

Finally, Parahunt stirred and the two rose up out of the water.

"This is the best thing you have taught me yet!" exclaimed Pepsi. "It is great fun!"

"Yes, but remember it can also save your life. When a lone man is on the run from his enemy, the river can provide safety."

Pepsi sat alone on his porch that evening. Although he was a loner by nature, his isolated lifestyle had taken some getting used to. Each night he read a chapter from his big Bible. And after reading, he would pray. He often thanked God for sending him a teacher like his Uncle Parahunt.

Summer turned into autumn, and autumn came with a vengeance. Parahunt did not visit for many weeks. And Pepsi grew lonely, but he was no longer afraid. He knew that word had gone out to all the native villages that he was under the special care of the mighty Parahunt, brother of Pocahontas.

Pepsi rode Brandy into Jamestown several times during the late fall. He was always glad to make it to a church meeting, or to visit with the Poythress family and, of course, Jane. And although he had many good friends in Jamestown, he still missed Parahunt's visits greatly. He began to wonder if his uncle was all right.

Finally on a frozen, snowy day in early winter, Parahunt returned. He explained that he had spent the past several weeks at his tribe's deer hunting camp in the mountains.

"There we hunt with a number of my clansmen. We surround the deer with huge rings of fire. It is the best way to get a lot of deer. This is so we can feed the many people of our tribe," he explained. "But there are deer near Varina, also. I will teach you the way of a single hunter."

First he showed Pepsicanough how to rub his clothes with the strong-smelling dried leaves Parahunt's daughters had prepared. This was the way to cover the man-smell. Then Pepsi stood proud as Parahunt covered him in an entire deerskin. The head of the deer fit right on his head, and the horns stood up to make a perfect disguise!

That day, he stalked through the forest wearing the deer skin and silent moccasins. At last, he crept close enough to a buck to bring it down with only a single arrow and a hunting knife. He stood before his trophy and grinned with pleasure, but seeing Parahunt's beaming face was even better.

Parahunt wore the proud look of a father. "You have done well, Pepsi. You are almost ready for *Huskanaw*," he announced.

"*Huskanaw?*" Pepsi was not familiar with this word.

"The Algonquin rites of manhood."

With such praise from this mighty warrior chief, Pepsi felt as if he were seven feet tall.

CHAPTER TWELVE

JANE

PEPSI SWUNG HIS AX HIGH over his shoulder, then with a mighty blow the sturdy log split neatly into two pieces. As he bent down to pick them up, he saw a movement in the distance. He slowly stood, and grinned when he recognized the form of his neighbor. Pepsi waved and called out a greeting, his breath coming out in steamy puffs as it met the freezing air.

"Hail, neighbor," called Master Gookin from the back of the loaded horse. "I have just returned from Jamestown with supplies."

"Climb down and come warm yourself by my fire," offered Pepsi. He led Master Gookin into his house and tossed a fresh log into the flames. He lifted the hot kettle of water from the fire and brewed a pot of native tea.

"Thank you, Thomas," said Gookin, taking a long sip.

"You look pale, neighbor," said Pepsi with concern.

"Yes, I have been plagued with the shaking sickness since summer. You know, your mother's people call late summer the Dying Season. But for us English, I think these cold damp winters are even more of a dying season." Gookin broke out coughing before he could finish. "Why, just this morning in Jamestown, I heard the dear Poythress girl is sick and close to death—"

"Miss Poythress?" Pepsi stood so quickly his cup clattered to the table. "She is sick?"

"Why, yes, Thomas, that is what I was told."

Already, Pepsi was pulling on his coat and the fur hat he had bought from a trapper. "Please excuse me, Master Gookin. Stay as long as you like, but I must go check on the Poythress family."

He bolted out the door and ran to saddle Brandy. At the stone storehouse, he quickly stopped and untied a hanging slab of frozen venison. He threw it over his horse and jumped into the saddle. He wished he could bring something more; if only he had some of Parahunt's healing herbs and ointments. But all he could think was that Mr. Gookin had said Jane was near death! He must get to her! He must see her! He pressed Brandy forward against the freezing wind.

"Please, Lord, please," he prayed. "Give Your strength to Jane."

It was dark by the time he galloped into Jamestown. He jumped down from his horse and burst into the Poythress house, even forgetting to knock. The front parlor room was dark and still, but a light shone from the cooking room.

"Hello," he called quietly. "Is anyone home?"

A serving girl poked her head out in surprise. "Can I help you, master?"

"I have heard that Miss Poythress is ill," he said urgently.

"Yes, sir, the lassie is sick nigh unto death. For three days, her father and mother have sat by her bedside."

"Please," he begged. "Please take me to her."

He followed the maid's raised candle up the steep stairs. He felt his heart in his throat—would he even be able to speak? And what would he say to his dear Jane? They entered a small bedroom beneath the thatched roof, and the maid stepped aside. His eyes flew to the bed and focused upon the pale little face with closed eyes that lay there.

But this was not his Jane! He recognized the youngest of the Poythress daughters—poor little Ruth! Jane stood beside the bed, her back to Pepsi. She dipped a cloth into a basin of water, and then tenderly touched it to her little sister's forehead. Her weary father and mother sat nearby with heads bowed.

"Jane!" whispered Pepsi. "When I was told that Miss Poythress was ill, I...I thought they meant you."

Jane turned around and her parents looked up with startled faces.

"Oh, Thomas Pepsi, how very kind of you to come. I have been ill, but not nearly as ill as our dear little Ruth." Jane came forward and touched his arm.

"I had to come," Pepsi said. He wanted to say more, to tell her how important she was to him. But the words were stuck in his throat.

For several days, Pepsi stayed next door at the fort barracks. But every waking moment was spent helping the Poythress family. He split several months' supply of firewood and stacked it neatly against the house. One night, he helped the serving girl to cook a thick, peppery stew from the venison he had brought. That same night, little Ruthie began to feel better. She asked for food, and Pepsi's stew was the first thing she had eaten for days.

The next day, the doctor came and proclaimed that Ruthie was "out of the woods"—she was going to live! It was almost miraculous, and the Poythress family and Pepsi all thanked God for her recovery. Pepsi heard that others in Jamestown were not so fortunate. He continued to help out the family, but by the end of the week, he knew it was time to return home.

Winter was the loneliest time of year at Varina. Parahunt seldom came to visit, and the isolation was sometimes almost too much to bear. Pepsi tried to busy himself with woodworking projects and reading, but sometimes he longed for the sound of a human voice. One cold foggy day, he sat alone before his fire and carved on a nice piece of oak. Suddenly his knife stopped and he paused to listen—was someone shouting outside? He leaped from his chair and ran to the window in time to see three bundled figures approaching his house.

"Hello! Hello! Thomas Pepsi, are you there?"

He threw open the door and welcomed Colonel Poythress and Jane. They were accompanied by another man whom Pepsi had never met.

"We have come to bring you back to the fort for Christmas chapel and dinner," the colonel announced firmly.

Christmas? Pepsi realized that he had lost track of time.

"And let me introduce our companion," the colonel continued. "A man who has been most anxious to meet you. This is Captain Henry Spelman."

Henry Spelman! Pepsi knew the name well. This was the same English boy who had lived in Werowocomoco, the one his mother saved from a murderous plan by an old priest. She had led him to safety and provided a home with the Potomacs. Only now, he was no longer a boy. Pepsi knew Henry must be about twelve years older than himself.

"I am very glad to make your acquaintance," Henry said,

warmly shaking his hand. "I will always be thankful for everything your mother did for me. Without her, I would not be alive today." Spelman continued to tell Pepsi how he worked as an interpreter between the colonists and the natives. Pepsi realized that Henry was much like himself—he also must live between two worlds.

As Henry spoke, Colonel Poythress stood quietly. Pepsi watched the colonel's eyes roaming around the room, taking in the tomahawk, the native traps, and the many animal skins that were scattered over the floor.

"I see that you have been in touch with your Indian relatives," the colonel said. His voice sounded cool and reserved, with just a trace of concern. "Do you not know, Thomas Rolfe, that since the Massacre of '22, it is illegal for a colonist to go to the tribesmen without written permission?"

"Yes, sir, I know that," answered Pepsi. "I did not go to the Algonquin. My uncle, Chief Parahunt, comes to me. Last summer, he saved my life. I was nearly drowned in the river. Parahunt teaches me many good things. Things that could be of use to the settlers of Virginia."

The colonel's only answer was a frown.

"Thomas," interrupted Henry. "It looks like you are getting along far better in the Algonquin training than I ever did. And I lived with the tribe for several years after Pocahontas rescued me."

"Enough talk." Jane's words were softened by her smile. "Pack up some things, Pepsi. You must come back with us for Christmas."

How could he say no to Jane? Besides, he was eager for human companionship; he had no intention of refusing this kind offer. He packed up a few things in his saddlebags, and secured them to his saddle.

As he was about to mount Brandy, he quickly turned and ran back into the house. He opened the heavy lid of his trunk. "Christmas is a time for special presents," he murmured.

The Poythress home was rustic but cozy, situated on the edge of the fort wall. Mrs. Poythress cooked a fine Canadian goose, and there was thick gravy for the native potatoes, and a fruit still new to the English settlers, called cranberries.

Christmas dinner was one of the most enjoyable times Pepsi could remember. He sat next to Jane, but tried not to talk too often. He didn't want to overwhelm her, but he had so much he wanted to share.

At one end of the table sat the friendly Captain Spelman. Over pumpkin custard, Henry told details of how Pocahontas had rescued him from the murderous Quiyow, and about living among the natives of the Potomac under her protection. Henry also described the day that Pocahontas was baptized. "That was when she took the name, Rebecca. Everyone admired her greatly, and it was plain for all to see that her faith was unshakable and sure."

It was a wonderful Christmas story—a story of what Christ's life meant to a young woman's heart. Pepsi again felt a swell of pride and love for the mother he had known so briefly, but who continued to live on in the hearts of many.

"Say, young Rolfe," said Colonel Poythress, interrupting his thoughts. "Word has it that you were quite a swordsman back in Cambridge. There above the fireplace hang my sabers. Why don't you and Captain Spelman here, give us an after-dinner demonstration? My young children would surely enjoy it!"

Henry and Pepsi both stood, and cleared an open space in the keeping room for some good-natured sword play. They picked up the swords and, with careful precision, they lunged and turned and posed; then lunged and turned again.

Jane's littlest sister, Nettie, sat on the floor, laughing and clapping at every parry. Young Ruth was still very weak, but wrapped snugly in a knitted shawl, she sat in a chair by the fire and smiled. Jane stood nearby, applauding the fencing with her sisters. Pepsi felt her eyes follow his every move.

Finally the demonstration drew to an end, and Henry thanked the Poythress family and said it was time for him to return to his barracks. Nodding toward Jane, Pepsi asked if he might be excused to step into the cool night air with Henry.

"Perhaps I could join you," suggested Jane shyly. "I too would appreciate a breath of fresh air." She pulled on a heavy velvet cloak and slipped the hood over her thick curls. They stepped outside with Captain Spelman. But Henry winked at Pepsi, then smiled and waved good night.

Jane and Pepsi stood together looking up at the shining crystal stars. The snow on the ground gave muffled silence to the already quiet night.

"I pray that Jamestown can go on being as peaceful as it is this wonderful night," said Jane.

"I pray that, too," he answered.

"There are rumors that Chief Opech is planning another uprising. Henry Spelman brought this horrible news to my father." Jane sighed. "Oh, Pepsi, can you not go to him? You once told me that he has asked to see you. You are the son of the beloved Pocahontas. Surely he would listen to you…"

"I will never go to him, Jane," Pepsi shook his head. "You

know I have hated the name of Opech since the death of my father. How could I even look at him without wanting to lunge forward to kill him? I fear I would not only bring about my own death, but I would surely bring his wrath upon all of Jamestown! I'm sorry, Jane, I don't feel I will ever be able to forgive my uncle Opech. It would be like forgiving the devil himself!"

"I understand." For a long moment she stood silent at his side, but then she spoke. "But maybe, Pepsi—maybe forgiveness can be an action, and not just a feeling. Maybe God wants us to act with forgiveness, even if we do not *feel* forgiving."

"I don't think I understand, Jane." He paused. "But I promise to consider your words."

She looked up and smiled, and when he saw her illuminated by the starlight, he felt certain the warmth of her face could melt even the icy snow and bring springtime again.

He smiled down at her. "At least I have been restored to one member of my family, Jane. My uncle Parahunt has taught me so many useful things. He is even teaching me Algonquin words." He paused and studied her face, wondering if he should continue to say what was in his heart. Again she smiled, and he continued. "And I have learned a very special word. It is a very long one: *noowomantain-moonkam-nonash.*"

"*Noowomantain-moonkam-nonash,*" she repeated slowly. "I have never heard this word. What does it mean?"

"It means *my love,*" he said gently. She stood silently, but her eyes sparkled with an answer that he understood.

Pepsi reached into his coat pocket and removed the only gift he had wanted to give to Jane for Christmas. He had been unsure if he would even get the chance, but now he knew the time had come. He handed her a small package wrapped in a piece of lace cloth—the package that had been stored in his trunk for so many years.

"Merry Christmas, Jane," he said quietly, his voice choked with emotion. She carefully unwrapped the lace and opened the small package to find his mother's beautiful pearl earrings. A soft gasp escaped her lips and she looked up with tears in her eyes.

"I have told you that these earrings, that once belonged to the Princess Pocahontas, would one day belong to my wife," Pepsi whispered. "I want that to be you, Jane."

"Oh, Thomas Pepsi, I want to accept your gift and the invitation that it represents. With all my heart," she whispered. "But you know that our engagement must also be permitted by my father."

"Yes, Jane, I hope to speak with your father tomorrow. But I admit, I feel the same kind of tension I felt that day back in England when I got ready to wrestle that bear!"

The next morning, after spending the night at the barracks, Pepsi returned to the Poythress home. Mustering all of his courage, he requested to speak with the colonel alone in his study.

"Sir, I have come to ask permission to court your daughter," he said quickly, hoping to get this session over with. He swallowed hard and looked directly into the older man's eyes.

"I have seen this coming," said the colonel thoughtfully. "And I must say that ever since the day I first met you in Scotland long ago, I have known that you are a fine lad, Thomas Rolfe."

"Then we have your blessing?" Pepsi continued eagerly. "I know that right now I do not have much of this world's possessions to offer. But I am working hard at Varina. Someday it will be a great plantation."

"I am afraid we live in troubled times, Thomas." The old man's face was lined with worry. "And I fear we cannot enter into a formal agreement or post the banns of engagement for a very long time."

Pepsi felt his heart hit the floor.

"I know you are committed to your land at Varina, but I can't let Jane marry you and move far from the safety of our soldiers here at Jamestown. Although it has been years since the massacre, we still have no treaty of peace. And right now rumors abound that your uncle, Chief Opech, is threatening another uprising."

Pepsi's head dropped down and he swallowed hard. Why did he suddenly feel somewhat responsible for the actions of his evil uncle? What could he possibly do to change that wicked man's heart?

"And to tell you the truth, Thomas," the colonel continued, "I do worry about your mixed Algonquin and English blood."

"Do you mean, sir, that you do not want Jane in a mixed marriage?" Pepsi was prepared for rejection, but he did not expect prejudice from the colonel.

"No, that is not my meaning, Thomas. I only worry that your mixed blood could make you something of a target if the tribe should go on the rampage again. Son, think of what that might mean for your wife and future children! Your own father's death should be lesson enough."

Pepsi nodded solemnly. And although he could form no words, he knew the colonel was right. He knew how it felt to lose his own father in a massacre like that. How could he risk Jane? It was one thing for him to live miles away from Jamestown in isolation; he did not worry much about putting himself in danger. But he could not do that to Jane.

He felt sad and foolish as he considered how only last night, he had been deliriously happy in the thought of his love for Jane. Now in the clear light of day, he understood the reason behind her father's refusal.

With a heavy heart, he said good-bye to Jane. He knew by her red-rimmed eyes that she too had heard the painful news. He traveled the long, lonely path back to Varina. Perhaps this was his lot in life. It seemed he was once again destined to be alone.

The first weeks of the new year were solitary ones for Thomas Pepsicanough Rolfe. Sometimes in the evenings he would bring Lightning from her roost in the barn. He had built her an indoor perch and placed it in the coolest end of his sitting room. The falcon would turn her head and gaze at him as if asking him why he had brought her inside. And soon she would stretch and flap great her wings, and Pepsi would carry her back out to her roost. He knew it was silly to bring in a large bird of prey as a house companion.

The two people in the entire world that he felt the closest to were Jane and his uncle, Parahunt. It amazed and confused him that these two, who were dearest to his heart, lived in two very different worlds. Inside, he felt the pull of both his English blood and his Algonquin blood. And sometimes during those dreary days of winter, he felt his love for the two sides would rip him apart.

He knew he was welcome to return to the fort, and that he could live safely as an Englishman. If he promised to settle there, and have nothing to do with his Algonquin uncle, the colonel might think him a safe match for Jane.

Or he could accept Parahunt's invitation to come and live in the safety of the Algonquin village. Pepsi could not deny that he felt a growing admiration for the life that Parahunt led. But to adopt the Algonquin way of life was to give up Jane forever. To choose either of these worlds meant to completely lose the other. And not only that, but how could he leave behind Varina, the place that had been so loved by both his mother and father?

Thomas Pepsi rode into Jamestown for supplies one day toward the end of winter. He spotted Jane from a distance. But he did not allow himself to go and speak with her. It would be too painful for them both. On his way back to Varina, he began to pray. He pleaded with God to give him some kind of answer to his confusion. He asked God to show him which way to go. As he prayed he remembered something John Eliot had once said: *God always answers our prayers. But often the answers are different than what we expect.*

CHAPTER THIRTEEN

NEW MISSIONARIES

IT WAS LATE MARCH, and the force of nature had finally broken the cold winter spell. Spring had come to the Chesapeake! Tiny green sprouts pushed aside the cold soil and rock, and reached hopefully up to the sun. The days lengthened, and the red-winged blackbirds came home. Pepsi's land of Varina exploded in wildflowers, honeysuckle and lilacs. Even the rosebushes his father had planted under his windows were growing. It was planting time!

"Now I know why Father wrote to me and said that Virginia was the fairest of all lands," Pepsi said aloud to his plowing partner—his horse, Brandy.

He stopped to wipe the sweat from his forehead at the end of a long plowed row. He glanced toward the river, and noticed a barge come into view. It was Mr. Gookin with several other men. One of the men frantically waved his hat at Pepsi. Something about that motion looked familiar. Could it possibly be?

"John Eliot!" Pepsi shouted as he raced to the dock. "John Eliot!" he yelled again and again. He leaped onto the barge. It was a fantastic reunion of back slapping and exclamations.

When Mr. Gookin could finally get in a word, he introduced the other men on the barge. "This is my son, Daniel, whom I am mighty proud of. Daniel has been living up in the Massachusetts Bay Company and he's the traveling companion of the Reverend Eliot. I was so surprised to learn that you and the Reverend are old friends."

Daniel was square and solid like his father, and built like an English bulldog. He looked slightly older than Pepsi, and wore knee-high fringed moccasins just like Pepsi. Daniel had the look of a real frontiersman.

"And this is Reverend Eliot's other traveling companion, Chanico," Mr. Gookin said. "Chanico is from Jamestown. From Opech's village before that. Chanico was in Jamestown on the day of the great massacre. Had he not warned his adopted family, many more of Jamestown's people would have been killed."

"After that day, Chanico left Jamestown," explained John Eliot. "He sought a new home with a Christian family in Massachusetts Bay. Now we travel together, and he's helping me to learn the Algonquian language."

"Well, I must continue on my way," said Mr. Gookin. "I leave these good men in your care, Thomas."

"Come on up to my house, all of you," invited Pepsi. "Join me for some cider."

"I pastor my own congregation now, Thomas," said John as they sat at the rough-hewn table drinking cool cider. "It's in Roxbury, Massachusetts. And I have married my sweetheart, Hannah. We are very happy. She understands my desire to reach out to the native people. During the week, I travel through the wilderness with Chanico and Daniel Gookin. Then I return to the pulpit on Sundays."

John walked across the room to where Pepsi's very special King James Bible lay open on the table. He picked it up reverently. "I have a new vision for my life," John confided. "I am going to translate the Bible into Algonquian."

"That is an impossible dream!" exclaimed Pepsi. "The common man only has Scripture in English, German and Dutch. And these versions were translated by many scholars. The Algonquins don't even have any kind of written language or alphabet—"

"I know these things, my friend. But with Daniel and Chanico at my side, and by the grace of the Almighty, I plan to translate the whole of the Bible into the Algonquian tongue," John smiled.

"And there is a way you can help us, my friend." John's eyes were as piercing as the falcon Lightning's.

"Me?" Pepsi asked.

"We need to find out which of the Powhatan villages might be the most accepting of our work. Chanico says the great Chieftess Cleopatre, your mother's sister, has been open to the Gospel teaching in the past. We want you to go with us to her village, Thomas. Then we can ask her opinion about our travels and our work."

"I know that Cleopatre is the ruler of a large village, and Parahunt had told me that she is one of my relatives. But how do you know she is open to hearing the Gospel?" Pepsi was confused.

Chanico spoke up. "Chieftess Cleopatre is the daughter of Powhatan. She was called Matachanna Kahnessa in her youth.

Do you not remember? She is your mother's sister; she went with you on the journey to England. This is the woman who cared for you, Pepsicanough, when you were a baby. This woman understood the faith that was in your mother's heart."

Pepsi was amazed. "I did not know that Cleopatre was the same sister who I remember as Aunt Kahnessa...."

John Eliot looked at Pepsi, and spoke with calm certainty, "God will weave all these threads from your past into His Great Plan."

There was a short silence. "I will go," Pepsi said firmly.

The three men stayed the night at Varina. The next morning, they arose and departed before the sun came up.

Pepsi and Chanico led the way, followed closely by John and Daniel. The four of them marched quickly and steadily uphill on the path that led to Cleopatre's village of Mattaponi. The trail seemed like only a deer path to Pepsi, but Chanico was sure of the way. The friends hiked for ten hours, stopping only for water and the dried fish which Pepsi had brought.

Warning drums echoed through the woods long before they reached the village. Chanico met a runner, and sent him back to the village with word to Cleopatre about her nephew's visit. Soon curious men and women began to line their path, and by the time they crossed through several fields of maize, at least a dozen giggling naked children ran ahead of them, followed by barking puppies.

Finally they came to the roaring waterfall of the Chickahominy River, and nearby rose the walls of Mattaponi. Pepsi and his friends approached the gate. Would they be welcome? They were ushered through and found themselves in a village of over fifty wigwams. In the center of the village stood a tall ceremonial pole decorated with strange symbols.

A regal delegation awaited them, led by a giant of a man. He was almost seven feet tall, and his face and arms were painted red. His hair was shaved on the right side, braided on the left, and stood up stiffly on top. "I am Remcoe, husband of the great Spirit Woman, Cleopatre," he said in a deep voice. "Follow me, Pepsicanough."

Pepsi did not know what to expect when he pushed through the hide-covered door of the Spirit Woman's longhouse. He strained his eyes in the smoky dimness, and looked toward a great fur-covered, throne-like platform. But she wasn't there. Instead he was surprised by the large Algonquin woman who rushed forward with outstretched arms.

"My sister's child! My Pepsicanough!" she murmured in Algonquian. "How I have longed to see you again!"

He found himself embraced in a tight bear hug. Aunt Cleopatre had added weight to her height since he'd last seen her. She was smiling and tears of joy were streaming down her round cheeks. He always thought his mother's people never showed such emotions. Apparently this wasn't so with the women! Aunt Cleopatre clung to him like a fierce mother bear who had just found a long-lost cub. She patted his cheeks and squeezed his muscled arms. "You are a strong boy," she proclaimed. "A good, strong boy."

Pepsi was stunned, not only by the emotional welcome, but also by his aunt's warm and genuine love. He had only a vague memory of Kahnessa as a young woman. She looked much different now. Her hair was gray, and when she grinned, he saw that she had more toes than teeth!

She locked her arm in his, and led him around the village for a tour. She motioned for John, Daniel, and Chanico to follow. They visited wigwam after wigwam, nodding after each Algonquin name was spoken.

One wigwam served as the royal storehouse for trade goods, extra corn and food supplies. Cleopatre gave the young man at the door a command that Pepsi could not quite understand. He thought he heard her say something about a *papoose*, the Algonquian word for baby.

Then from the back of the storehouse, the young man brought forth a long bundle wrapped in soft deerskin. Big Cleopatre held it lovingly, and carefully unwrapped it for Pepsi and his friends to see. It was an Algonquin baby carrier!

"This, Pepsicanough, was your first cradle-board, from when you were a tiny papoose. I made it for you when you were born, but your dear mother did all the beadwork. Of course, you outgrew this first one quickly. But I have saved it for you here, as is our custom. I will bring it to you one day, when *your* first child is born!"

Pepsi was amazed. Here in this village, where he had never even lived, his aunt had faithfully guarded a keepsake from his baby days. He had vowed to forget the Chesapeake after his father's death—to forget his people here. But they had not forgotten him.

That night, Pepsi and his three friends were treated to a delicious feast in the royal longhouse. They dined on smoked trout, corn cakes, and dozens of other native dishes. Aunt Cleopatre made him sit right beside her on her wide, fur-covered platform. The longhouse was filled with all of the important people of the village.

"I would have come sooner," Pepsi explained in careful Algonquian. "But I did not realize that the Aunt Matachanna Kahnessa who cared for me when I was a baby, and who also went with us to England, had changed to Aunt Cleopatre!"

"Oh, I will tell you the reason," the Chieftess laughed deeply. "In England, have you not heard of the ancient woman queen named Cleopatra? I liked her name when I heard it, and so I took it for my own!"

"I see," said Pepsi. And he too began to laugh. It was impossible not to laugh around this warm, earthy queen-mother.

Later that night, the talk grew more serious. Pepsi asked Cleopatre about her feelings about the Christian's God.

"Oh, Cleopatre has good feelings toward this God. Pocahontas told me much of Him." She stopped suddenly, and Pepsi could see that she was trying to recall something. "Now, tell me the story of the saint you call Patrick!"

Pepsi was amazed. "Saint Patrick?"

"Yes," Cleopatre was firm. "This was your father's favorite story. He told it to me himself. He said the people far to the north of England—the people he came from—had once worshiped dark gods like the gods of the Quiyow. John Rolfe said that his ancestors even made human sacrifices before this Saint Patrick came to teach them. Do you not know this story, Pepsicanough?"

"Why, yes, of course I know it. I just did not know it was my father's favorite," he answered. Then, in his slow Algonquian, he tried his best to tell the story of the great missionary named Saint Patrick.

Cleopatre closed her eyes as he spoke. When he finished, her almost toothless grin was the most wonderful thank-you he could have received. Then Pepsi explained why John Eliot,

Chanico and Daniel had come with him. He told of their dream of putting the Algonquian language into writing, and how they longed to share God's message.

"Which village do you think might be most open to our visits, Cleopatre?" asked John Eliot. "Are there any that would like to learn of the Christian God?"

"I think you would be safe among the Wampanoegs," she said to John. "And I know you would be safe among the Potomacs." She went on to list more villages by name. "But do not go to the confederacy of Opech's villages. He worships only Okewas, the war god. Pepsicanough alone could stand before Opech."

John Eliot looked long and hard at Pepsi. And Pepsi remembered his vow of revenge—his promise to kill his uncle. He also remembered his vow to never return to the Chesapeake. Could God change his heart again?

Pepsi finally spoke up. "Long ago, I received a message that Opech had invited me to come to him and claim my inheritance. But I always believed it was a trick. I suspected that Chief Opech would kill me if I went to him."

Cleopatre grunted. "The invitation is no trick. Opech is head chief, but all Powhatan village chiefs know the great Chief Powhatan loved your mother. When you were born, Powhatan declared that *you* would be Chief. Opech must honor this. All chiefs who sit on the great council—and I am one of them—will hold him to Powhatan's will."

Pepsi nodded soberly. But a war raged inside him.

"Of course," the wise woman acknowledged, "Opech may think you are a weak English boy who will not survive the initiation of the Huskanaw. If you die in the initiation, Opech can claim that he *tried* to honor Powhatan's wish."

Pepsi said no more. He had just told his aunt the story of Saint Patrick. This godly man had returned to the Irish even though they kidnapped and enslaved him as a boy. How could Pepsi tell Cleopatre he would not go to Opech, because he could never overcome the hatred and revenge in his own heart? Even though he was a Christian, did they also expect him to be a *saint?*

With Cleopatre's permission, Chanico stood and told the story of Creator God and his son Jesus. Everyone listened with hushed attention. When Chanico finished, an old man stood and spoke.

"I am Wannalancet. In all my days, I have passed through the world in an old canoe. Now you tell me to leave my old canoe and embark in a new one. Before, I was unwilling. But now I yield myself up to your advice, and I enter into this new canoe. From hereafter, I promise to pray to a new God."

*   *   *

The next morning, Aunt Cleopatre took Pepsi for a walk along the river, and past the waterfall to where the Mattaponi River met the Pamunky River in a powerful torrent of crashing white water. His old aunt grew thoughtful as she looked at the roaring rivers melding before them.

"Here then is your name, Pepsicanough," she said with solemnness.

"What do you mean? I know nothing about my Algonquin name. I have never understood its meaning."

"Your name was given to you by your grandfather, the mighty Powhatan," she explained. "Your name, Pepsicanough, is a prophecy. Your name means *the joining place of two mighty rivers.*

"Look before you," she commanded. "See the great turmoil where the two rivers join. But soon, the Two Mighty Rivers become one. They join to become one river far more powerful than before."

He stared at the rushing waters and considered her words. So this was the prophecy for Thomas Pepsicanough Rolfe. He had felt the turmoil of the Algonquin and English rivers rushing inside of him, but perhaps someday they would flow smoothly into one river that was strong and free.

CHAPTER FOURTEEN

THE THIEF

THE JULY SUN BEAT DOWN without mercy. The Chesapeake baked after weeks without rain. Pepsi stood up from the row of Indian corn he was watering from a bucket and wiped his forehead on his sleeve. He hadn't been able to put in too many acres, but at least his crops were growing well so far. But how long could they last without rain?

As he surveyed the long, straight corn rows, he noticed two riders at the edge of his field. One rode side-saddle, with her long skirt and red curls blowing free. He recognized Jane, but who was that with her?

"I am glad to see you, Miss Poythress," said Pepsi, walking toward them. "It has been a very long time." He could see now that the other rider was a teenage boy, younger than himself.

"Yes it has, Pepsi, it has been months. But I hope not so long that you have forgotten to call me Jane!" She smiled, and Pepsi could not keep from smiling back. "This is Kevin O'Reilly," she motioned to the skinny boy at her side. "He is thirteen and a good worker. He was living with his uncle and helping to farm, but his uncle died recently of the shaking sickness. Now Kevin has no place to go, and I thought of Varina. I thought maybe with all of your work you could use his help. And Kevin could use a good place to stay."

"I will work hard for you." Kevin spoke with a thick Irish accent. Pepsi liked the honest way the lad looked him in the eye.

"This is a great idea, Jane," he answered. He turned to Kevin. "I would be glad to have your help." The boy broke into a wide grin, and Jane's smile was warmer than the sunshine. Pepsi invited them into the house. Jane and Kevin sat at his table as he served them a simple meal of squirrel, hardtack bread, and cold water from his well.

"Did Lightning find this lunch—or did you?" teased Jane.

Pepsi laughed. "It was Lightning. She's still a better hunter than I am!" While they were still eating, Pepsi heard the high-pitched warning scream of his falcon. The screech came again and again. Pepsi ran out the door. "Fire!" he yelled. "My fields are on fire!"

Smoke billowed as flames leaped from plant to plant. Pepsi grabbed a blanket and ran to beat the flames the way that Parahunt had taught him. Jane and Kevin joined him, stamping and kicking dirt onto the little tongues of fire. Then Pepsi heard Brandy whinny in panic.

"She's tied at the end of the field!" yelled Pepsi.

"I'll get her," Jane yelled back. She ran toward the frightened animal.

"Go help Jane!" Pepsi commanded Kevin. "That plow horse is too strong for her!" He kept beating the flames, throwing every ounce of strength into this battle. It looked like he was winning! The crops were still green enough to resist the flames. Maybe all was not lost. But then he heard a scream—a piercing scream that cut to his heart.

"Pepsi! Help, Pepsi!"

It was Jane! And she was in danger! As Pepsi ran toward her, he saw the horrible picture. A powerful warrior in war paint held Brandy's reins in one hand, and with the other hand he pinned Jane's arms behind her back and pushed her along before him. The man was quickly moving both the horse and Jane toward the forest.

In an instant, Pepsi sprang back for a weapon. There was not time to ready the gun—instead he grabbed Parahunt's tomahawk from its holder and raced through the field after the attacker. When he reached the edge of the field, he saw Kevin lying on the ground, bleeding. He knew now that the fire in the field had been a trick. The Indian was after his horse. Horses were still rare in the Chesapeake. And now that thief had also captured Jane!

Pepsi followed the thief's trail into the forest. It was obvious from the torn-up path that Jane was putting up a struggle, and even Brandy was proving hard to handle. Pepsi knew they could not have gotten far. Finally he spotted them. Jane had fallen to the ground and the thief was jerking on Brandy's reins.

Pepsi ran at full force from behind, his moccasins giving him noiseless speed. The attacker was about thirty feet ahead when Pepsi hurled the tomahawk. It flew perfectly, end over end, true to its mark. The weapon smacked the kidnapper's head with a sickening thud; the thief fell and lay still.

"Jane!" yelled Pepsi. "Jane, are you all right?" He ran to help her up from the ground.

"I'm all right, truly I am," she cried. "But, Pepsi, is Kevin alive?"

He put his arm around her and they hurried back to the

fence line. Kevin was covered with blood. But his eyes were still open as he lay on the ground moaning. He had been badly stabbed through the shoulder. Pepsi pressed hard on the wound to stop the bleeding. He stooped down to carefully lift the boy, then carried him back to the house. He lay Kevin on the table and instructed Jane to tear bandages from a clean tablecloth. Suddenly a great shadow appeared in the doorway and Jane screamed in horror.

"Parahunt!" cried Pepsi. "I'm so glad you're here!"

"I have seen the smoke of your fields," said Parahunt. "I have come to help you."

When Kevin's wounds were bound, Pepsi left Jane at the house to care for the boy. He led Parahunt to the place in the forest where the attacker had fallen.

Parahunt squatted and placed his hand on the man's heart. "He is not dead. He may not survive the blow of the tomahawk, but he is not yet dead."

"Where is he from?" asked Pepsi. He studied the man's clothing and tattoos. "Is he from the Chickahominy tribe?"

"No," said Parahunt. "This man is from a village of Powhatan. I do not recognize his face, but his appearance and painting is of the village where Opech now rules."

It was the worst thing Parahunt could have said. Pepsi was shocked to discover he had struck down an Algonquin from the very village of the cruel Chief Opech. No matter what the reason—even if the warrior was caught stealing a horse—Opech could now use this as an excuse to attack, not only Varina, but Jamestown and the homes of the other settlers as well. Pepsi knew that an incident like this had sparked the Massacre of '22.

Pepsi fell to his knees. "Opech will surely want to take

revenge," he muttered hopelessly.

"Get up, Pepsicanough," commanded Parahunt. "There is only one thing to be done. *You* must take this man to Opech."

Pepsi nodded. He knew his uncle was right. Even if Opech chose to kill Pepsi, it would be worth it, if his death could prevent an even worse massacre. He walked over and picked up Brandy's reins, resolved to do the right thing.

"Throw the Powhatan across your horse, and ride quickly while he still lives. Let Opech hear from your own mouth that this man was stealing your horse and your woman. Do not wait until he hears the news another way."

Pepsi picked up the unconscious attacker and slung him over Brandy's back, then slowly mounted behind the limp body.

"If you go face to face with Opech, he may give you Algonquin justice," advised Parahunt. "If not, there is nothing that will save you or others from his fury. I will stay here and see to the wounded boy and the lady." Parahunt gave some simple directions on how to find Werowocomoco. And Pepsi clicked his knees against Brandy's side and hurried up the path. He didn't expect justice from the detested Opech. But what else was there to do? Perhaps by going straight to Opech, he would spare Jane and the others from a full-scale tribal attack.

Only moments ago, he had been freely chatting with Jane out in his corn field; life had been full of joy and promise. Now he was on what seemed to be a hopeless mission. "I tomahawked a man from Opech's village," Pepsi said aloud in disbelief. "I am a dead man."

CHAPTER FIFTEEN

THE OATH OF OPECH

THE WOUNDED ATTACKER never moved during the two-hour ride, but Pepsi could see he was still breathing. The path led up the James River and across the Henrico peninsula. As he rode, Pepsi saw the blackened shells of buildings that had once housed both English and Indians. This was where his mother had first met his father, and where his father had died in the massacre that left only these fire-scarred remnants.

The river grew loud with the rapids, and soon he heard the pounding sound of the James River Falls. Here he would find the village of Werowocomoco, the village that white men simply called Powhatan, after his grandfather. His mother had been born here. But what had once been his grandfather's stronghold had now become the capital of the evil Chief Opech's domain.

Just as the guarded gate of the village came into sight, the thief, still slumped over his horse, began to moan. At least Pepsi could not be accused of murder. Not yet anyway....

Without warning he was yanked backward from his horse and thrown roughly to the ground. A warrior lunged at him, and before Pepsi could offer a word of explanation, he was smacked across the side of the head with a club. Pepsi blinked his eyes to focus, his mind spinning with dizziness. Was this how it would all end? Women and children began to gather, poking at him with sticks and yelping like animals.

"I am Pepsicanough!" he shouted, struggling to his feet. "Pepsicanough, son of the Princess Pocahontas and grandson of the great Powhatan. I demand to see my uncle, Chief Opech!"

"Be silent!" a gravelly voice commanded.

Pepsi looked up to see the most frightening being he could imagine. He was clearly an old Quiyow, a powerful Spirit Man. The Quiyow was painted in black and red, and wore an evil headdress made from weasel heads and snakes. In his ears, live snakes were pinned like earrings, writhing and hideous.

"Bring him to Opech!" commanded the powerful Quiyow.

Pepsi was grabbed by tall warriors and dragged through the village. They took him to what appeared to be a temple. In one corner stood a huge carved statue of Okewas. This must be the god of war that Pepsi had heard of—the idol carried by the warriors when they went to battle. Bloodstains from many victims darkened the wood of the carved idol. Perhaps his own father's blood was there.

Near this idol stood an old man, his feet planted wide apart and arms crossed. His leathery face wore a dark scowl and his proud flat nose was held high. Pepsi knew this was his uncle, Chief Opech, but he was much more ancient than Pepsi had expected. And yet, his black eyes still smoldered and burned with fire.

Here then was the man whom Pepsi had hated and feared for so many years. Here was the chief who had given the evil order that led to the death of his father. Pepsi had expected Opech to look like a demon, but instead he found an old man with grey hair, and a face deeply creased with the wrinkles of many seasons.

"I am Opechcanough, uncle to your mother, Pocahontas. I see that you have finally come to me, Pepsicanough." Opech's voice was like the growl of an old mountain lion.

"I have come only to return a wounded Powhatan." Pepsi formed the words in Algonquian. "He fell at my own hand, struck by my own tomahawk. No other settler should suffer for my actions. But I had no choice in what happened today. This man set fire to my fields, then kidnapped a girl and my horse." Pepsi took a deep breath and waited for his uncle's rage.

For a long time there was no reaction. Opech stood in silence, studying him closely. Pepsi stared back without flinching. Finally, the old Quiyow shuffled to Opech's side and mumbled something Pepsi could not hear. Were they plotting to lay his head upon a sacrificial stone, the way they had with Captain Smith so long ago? Surely, under this evil man's rule, no one would dare to save Pepsi the way Pocahontas had done.

Opech began to speak, and Pepsi was surprised when his words were not filled with fury. "My Quiyow has told me that you have returned with the man called Rassaneck. This man is of no consequence, Pepsicanough. This man was driven from our village last winter. This man stole from his own people. I am not surprised he would try to steal your horse. You have done well to wound such a man."

Pepsi tried not to show his surprise. Could it be that in saving

Jane, he had struck down a native that was already an enemy of Opech? And now he received thanks instead of fury!

"Come to my longhouse, Pepsicanough, and we will smoke the *uppowoc* pipe," announced Opech. The chief marched from the temple, motioning for Pepsi to follow. The sun was low in the sky as they walked through the village.

At the longhouse they were met by Parahunt. He explained to Pepsi that he had paddled up the James in his sleek canoe. He also assured Pepsi that Kevin was better. Word had been sent to the colonel, and he would help Jane care for Kevin at Varina until he was strong enough to be moved to the fort.

As night came, Pepsicanough and Parahunt sat around a council fire beside Opechcanough and his elders. No words were spoken as the peace pipe was smoked and passed from one warrior to the next. Pepsi knew how to be silently thoughtful. This quietness was the council way. Captain John Smith had told him this long ago.

Finally, Opech was ready to speak. "Many moons ago, I made a promise to your grandfather, Chief Powhatan. Because of his love for your mother, Pocahontas, he chose to give her son much land. When you were born, he gave unto you the land in the forests, the land in the fields, and the land down to the Great Sea...." The old chief paused and Pepsi waited. A burning log on the council fire snapped and red embers drifted up through the smoke. Still Pepsi waited.

The old man continued. "When Powhatan lay dying, I swore to give Pepsicanough, the son of Pocahontas, the promised lands. I sent word to the Governor of the Virginia Company in Jamestown. I waited for you to come."

"I could not come sooner. The governors of the Virginia

Company did not believe you truly wanted to give me my land," answered Pepsi woodenly. "Many who have trusted you in the past have died." Pepsi spat out these last words. From across the council fire, Parahunt's eyes warned Pepsi to say no more.

Opech's face grew dark as he spoke. "And in return, I do not trust the white man. In the early days of Jamestown, it was the white man who killed two of my sons. I waited many years for my vengeance."

Pepsi considered these words. Was it true that the Massacre of '22 occured because Opech *himself* sought revenge? Pepsi had never heard this before. He had not known of the death of Opech's two sons.

Opech continued solemnly. "But still I am sworn to keep my word about *you*, Pepsicanough, for in you flows the blood of my brother Powhatan. It is right that you have finally come."

"My heart was not ready to come sooner," said Pepsi with honesty. In that same instant he remembered what Jane had told him: *God wants the act of forgiveness, even if you do not feel forgiving.* And suddenly a new idea began to form in his mind.

"I do not come to claim my land, Uncle Opech," he began slowly. "I have enough land in the place called Varina, the place where I was born. But I have decided to claim my rightful position as the son of Pocahontas. I have come to be named a chief, a leader among your people. This is my blood right!"

Opech sat in silence, his scowling face illuminated by the slow-burning flames. "You cannot become a chief unless you are first a warrior. And you cannot be an Algonquin warrior unless you first go through the Huskanaw."

Parahunt spoke quietly, "Pepsi knows this, Uncle."

"Then let the Huskanaw begin with the sunrise," said

Opech. And Pepsi nodded in agreement.

Parahunt and Pepsi slowly walked to the wigwam that housed visitors. Pepsi breathed deeply of the cool night air. Overhead, the stars burned brightly and Pepsi felt a small wave of hope wash over him.

"I am sure that Opech thinks the Huskanaw will kill you," said Parahunt. "He could not want you to sit at the council fires as a rightful chief of our people. He knows you will speak up for peace." Pepsi nodded, but he no longer felt the familiar anger toward Chief Opech.

Parahunt continued in a serious tone. "Many of our own boys do not survive the Huskanaw. But it is the only way for you to claim your rightful place among us, Pepsi. And I think you are ready. Perhaps the God of Pocahontas will help you."

Parahunt threw back the hide door of the round lodge where Pepsi was to sleep. "Pepsi, I brought your falcon in my canoe. You will not feel alone." The small fire illuminated the wigwam well enough to see the great bird upon her traveling perch. Lightning remained calm because of the dark hood covering her eyes. But Pepsi spoke soothing words to her anyway. Parahunt had been right to bring her. Somehow Pepsi *did* feel comfort from the closeness of his faithful hunting partner.

The next morning, Parahunt prepared Pepsi for the Huskanaw. First his head was shaved, and his English clothes were replaced by a breechcloth. Even his native moccasins were removed. Then Parahunt took him to the sweat lodge. A steam bath had been prepared, with sizzling hot round stones from firepits and river water. Pepsi and Parahunt stooped through the door and joined the other warriors. The men sat in a circle and chanted old warrior and hunting tales.

"Umm, bear claws!" said one old warrior. He knowingly traced his finger along the welts that Pepsi had received from the bear wrestling. The other Algonquin warriors looked upon Pepsi with respect.

Pepsi followed the example of the other men who stayed in the oppressive heat as long as they could. At that point, they burst from the lodge and jumped into the cool river. How good it felt! Pepsi dunked his head once again into the cool water, thankful to be done with this part of the Huskanaw.

"Pepsi," called Parahunt from the river bank. "It is time for you to return to the sweat lodge."

Pepsi looked up in surprise. "What do you mean, Uncle?"

"You must continue the steam bath alone now, Pepsi," instructed Parahunt. "You must complete this same process seven times."

By the time Pepsi finished the seventh steaming, he walked to the river on shaking legs. He felt completely weak and drained of strength. As he rested in the cool river water, Parahunt explained everything else that he was expected to do.

"You will go alone toward the Blue Haze Mountains, and there you will fast for seven days. During this time, you will purify your soul with prayer. After those seven fasting days, you can begin to eat the fruits and grains of nature, but no meats will enter your mouth. You will stay in the forest for fourteen more days. A man of the tribe will follow you throughout the whole time, to witness that you do not break the Huskanaw rules."

Parahunt shared more wisdom about fasting. He advised him about the terrain of the Blue Haze Mountains. And he also warned him about the dreaded Mohawks who roamed that area.

"During the last fourteen days, you must perform a great act of valor. You will kill a mighty beast like the mountain cougar. Or perhaps a warrior from an enemy tribe. Only after this true act of valor can you again eat meat." Parahunt showed Pepsi a long hunting knife. "This will be your only weapon."

Pepsi climbed out of the water and sat by Parahunt on the river bank. He felt tired, and hopeless, and hungry. But Parahunt continued to speak.

"When you return to the village, you will be given the Huskanaw vision-medicine. This is the herb-drug that your people call the Jimmy weed. It will bring you into a trance. At that time you will receive your vision from your Manitou. And you will dance all night with the elders. After that, Opech will call Pepsicanough a man, and worthy to become an Algonquin chief."

"Parahunt, I thank you for all you have done for me." Pepsi placed his hand on his uncle's shoulder. "I have one question. You have told me that many of the young men die during their Huskanaw. How do they die?"

A cloud passed over his uncle's face. "They die from weakness."

CHAPTER SIXTEEN

THE HUSKANAW

"GO WITH YOUR GOD," called Parahunt. Pepsi turned and waved, then followed the path to the village gate. His feet were still bare and he wore only a breechcloth. He was just outside of the village when he noticed a strange dark figure lurking in the shadows ahead.

The hair on his neck stood up when he realized it was the ancient Quiyow. The old spirit-man blocked his path, chanting loudly, his snake earrings writhing. Pepsi knew the chants were to curse his journey. But he also remembered how the old warrior, Tomoco, had worn live snakes like these on the ship that carried Pepsi's family to England. Those snakes had shriveled and died and finally been thrown into the sea.

Remember, our God is more powerful than the magic of Oke-was Mother had said all those years ago, as they watched the dead snakes be swept under the waves. Pepsi took a deep breath and stepped around the chanting Quiyow. He continued boldly up the trail that led to the north.

The first days of the Huskanaw were not bad days. He was hungry as he walked, but he could endure that. Parahunt had taught him that his spirit should rule his body. It grew cooler each night as he reached the higher elevations, but he welcomed the coolness after the blistering heat of the day. His feet ached with cuts and bruises. But he continued to walk and soon his feet became numb. On the fourth day, the effects of hunger began to wear on him. He grew dizzy and often stumbled as he walked. It was painful when he fell and often he felt he had no strength to get up and continue.

On fifth day he wanted to give up. He was crawling up a sun-baked stony ridge, barely moving an inch at a time. Two lazy shadows circled slowly around him, and he knew the hungry vultures were waiting for him to perish. He remembered what Parahunt had said about dying from weakness, and he knew he could never make it to the top. Even if he did make it—what then? "Help me, God," he whispered hoarsely.

He didn't know how, but he finally reached the top and slowly pulled himself to his feet and stared in wonder. There before him stretched a high mountain meadow, green and lush. And he heard the sound of rushing water. Was this for real, or only a mirage? He stumbled toward the water sound to discover a gurgling stream nearby. He fell to his stomach and plunged in his head, careful not to drink too much. Finally he sat up and stuck his swollen feet into the water. A movement on the other side of the meadow caught his eye, and he quickly spotted the Algonquin warrior who had been assigned to follow him. The older man came along to make sure that Pepsi did not break the Huskanaw vow. Or maybe to return to the village and tell them that Pepsi had died....

By mid-afternoon of the sixth day, he could walk no longer. He sat down under a tree and leaned his arms and head on his knees. He prayed. He slept. He prayed some more. He was so weak, he thought this might be the end.

In the early evening of the seventh day he heard a flock of geese flying overhead. He looked up and watched as they dipped down below a tall stand of pines. Then he forced himself to his feet and walked slowly in that direction. He hoped the geese had landed near water—he had not tasted water since yesterday. He stumbled through the wooded area and finally came upon a small mountain lake. He slipped down the bank and into the coolness of the lake. He allowed himself to drink a bit and then he lay back against the bank with the lower half of his body still submerged in the water.

Suddenly he heard the sound of voices nearby. Their words traveled easily across the calm water, and although he could hear them, he did not understand their language. He froze as still as a hunted woodland creature, and narrowed his eyes to focus on the natives who were walking around the lake in his direction.

They were Mohawks! Five of them! The haircuts and leggings were just as Parahunt had described. He noticed what appeared to be fresh scalps hanging from the belts of two of the warriors. This was clearly a war party, probably returning from a raid on the nearby Potomacs.

What could he do? In no condition to defend himself, he might be able to hide in the nearby trees, but if he stood, they would see him for sure.

Then it came to him—he remembered when Parahunt had taught him to hide in the river at Varina! Not far away, along the edge of the lake, grew tall reeds. He slid silently into the water, then swam below the surface the way Parahunt had taught him, until he reached the place where the reeds grew. He allowed his face to rise just above the water long enough to catch his breath and break off a long, hollow stem. Then he slipped totallv beneath the water and lay on his back, breathing slowly through the long green tube of the reed he held in his mouth.

Within minutes, he saw the shadowy figures of the Mohawks moving right past him along the bank! But he was well hidden in the thickness of the reeds, and they marched on by without even pausing. Once again, he thanked God for allowing Parahunt to show him these skills of survival! He lay under the water for a long time, unwilling to take any chances, but also enjoying the cool refreshment.

Even his hungry belly could not keep him awake on the seventh night. He found a bed in the crevice of a giant granite rock. He rolled up a ball of moss to use as a pillow. The warmth of the day's sun remained in the big stone to ward off the night's chill. He had survived the seven days of fasting. God was with him— he knew it!

The next morning he awoke with the sun. Today he could break his fast! He grabbed his hunting knife and used it to dig *polanti,* the long tuberous vegetable growing all around him. He found a loaded berry bush and grabbed handfuls of its sweetness. But he knew he must be careful. Parahunt had warned him that many grew ill from stuffing themselves after a fast—it could be worse than the actual fast. All that day and the next he ate small portions of whatever food he found, and then he rested. Slowly his strength returned. And he continued toward the mountains.

A deed of valor. That was his next challenge. If he continued into the mountains he might meet another Mohawk, but in his heart he knew he could not kill a man unless it was self-defense. One night he heard the distant screams of a mountain cougar, but by morning he could tell that it was too far away to track. He saw many great stags, and he knew he could probably kill one, but that did not seem valiant enough for the grandson of Powhatan.

Finally, in the third week of his Huskanaw, he saw the tracks of a bear. A massive bear. He began to follow them and soon found that something was wrong. The bear's path was strewn with damage. Branches were broken and small trees were uprooted. Pepsi had heard how a wounded bear will destroy anything in its path. He knew that nothing was more dangerous or unpredictable.

It took him several hours to catch up with the animal. He finally spotted the huge bear lumbering down a hillside. The wounded beast walked unevenly, dragging its right front leg. It could have been injured by falling into a covered pit, dug by a native for a bear trap. But whatever had happened, this huge animal was on the run—and angry!

Maybe it was foolish to try and fight such an animal. Hadn't he learned this lesson once before? Maybe he should look for another deed of valor. But as soon as this concern entered his mind, the mountain breeze shifted, and the giant bear lifted its nose and turned toward the hill. Suddenly, there was no decision—Pepsi was now the hunted one! The bear rose upon its hind feet and growled in fury, as if the smell of a hated human had enraged it. Then, with more speed than Pepsi thought possible, the bear tore up the hill.

Quick as a flash, he remembered the last time he fought a bear—he survived by rolling into a ball, and then caught the animal off-guard and leaped onto its back. Could that same technique work again? It was worth a try! He curled into a ball and lay still. The confused animal slowed down and let out a bone-chilling growl. Then with its good paw it gave Pepsi a crushing blow that sent him hurling down the hillside. When Pepsi stopped rolling, he lay curled on his side as still as a stone. As the bear approached, he slowly slipped his knife out of its snug leather holder.

This time the bear came close and paused. The bear was so close that Pepsi felt the fur brush against his left arm, and the smell was sickening. Pepsi focused himself for the next move; there wasn't a moment to lose. He rolled over and sprang up—and in the same instant he plunged the long knife deep into the heart of the bear.

The knife went true, but the bear's teeth still came down, ripping across Pepsi's shoulder in a wound that made him scream with pain. The bear growled again and Pepsi thought that he was a dead man. But at last, the animal slumped over and fell sideways.

Pepsi cleansed his wound in the mountain stream, and then placed an herbal medicine pack on it the way that Parahunt had once shown him. He then skinned the bear and rolled the great fur up to take back to Chief Opech. The Algonquin warrior, who had been sent to follow, stepped out of the forest shadows and into the clearing so that Pepsi could see him. The man waved his hand and then turned and walked south toward Werowocomoco. This must be the signal that this true act of valor would conclude Pepsi's Huskanaw. Pepsi looked up at the sky and thanked God.

That night, he cooked himself a huge bear-steak. He remembered the scolding John Smith had given him after the tomahawk lesson. Pepsi had not forgotten that an Algonquin only kills an animal for meat. He slept soundly that night and the next morning he headed south.

After several days of walking, he finally came to the river that led to the village. When the village gate came into view, he immediately spotted Parahunt sitting cross-legged beside the posts. He seemed to be waiting for him. Parahunt stood and greeted Pepsi, then examined the size of the bear's pelt. His uncle made no comment on the impressive trophy, but Pepsi recognized the pride in his eyes. They walked together into the village.

Pepsi knew one more step of the Huskanaw awaited. He was expected to take the hallucinating drug in order to experience a vision of his Manitou—his animal spirit. He had prayed about this on his trip back to the village. He knew the dangers of Jimmy weed and had finally decided not to partake of this drug. But how would he explain this decision to Opech? He prayed again that God would help him.

Early that evening, the village drums throbbed in a repetitive rhythm. Pepsi had been to the steam lodge for purification. And now his face and upper body were decorated in ceremonial patterns of red, yellow and black. He wore leather britches and his own knee-high moccasins. He stood before the large fire that burned in the center of the village. All around him stood tribal members, waiting to see Pepsi experience his Manitou. The warrior who had faithfully trailed and watched Pepsi during his Huskanaw now stepped forward to present Pepsi to Opech and the old Quiyow.

The Quiyow began to chant. Slowly at first, then faster and faster. Then a younger spiritman came forward and handed a shell bowl to the Quiyow. The Quiyow held the shell high and then placed it into Pepsi's hands. Pepsi looked down at the dark strong-smelling liquid. Suddenly, the drumming stopped. The village was silent. Everyone looked at the son of Pocahontas.

Pepsi prayed a silent prayer, then turned to the Quiyow. "I have fasted and prayed. I have gone out for the Huskanaw, and I have returned to bring Opech the pelt of a mighty bear that I killed with my own hands. But I cannot drink this." Pepsi chose his Algonquian words carefully. "I do not believe that I need this to have a vision."

Opech's eyes opened wide at the refusal of this drink, and the old Quiyow shook with anger. Pepsi knew that the insult was great. It might even be enough for them to kill him. But suddenly Parahunt was at his side.

"Pepsicanough is older than many of our boys who drink to receive their Manitou vision," said Parahunt in a calm voice. "Pepsicanough already has his Manitou. And his Manitou does not just appear to him once—it stays with him always!"

Pepsi stared at his uncle with amazement. He was talking about Lightning! He had Lightning for a Manitou!

"I will show you!" said Pepsi, trying to conceal his excitement. He hurried to the wigwam where Parahunt had been secretly keeping and feeding the great bird during Pepsi's absence. He untied her from the perch and carried her on his arm back to the gathering. Once again he stood beside Chief Opech. Gasps of unbelief rippled throughout the crowd. The Algonquins held eagles and other birds of prey in high esteem. And they had never before seen a trained one.

As Pepsi slipped off Lightning's leather hood, he realized that the design on it looked almost Algonquin. The tuft of feathers that stuck up at the top were yellow, red and black—just like the paint that decorated his own body.

He lifted his arm high in the signal, and Lightning took off with a flurry. Again the crowd murmured with awe as they followed her with their eyes. She had been cooped up for days and eagerly sought her freedom to soar. She beat her wings against the air and sailed upward over the village, higher and higher. The villagers shaded their eyes in order to glimpse Lightning's silhouette against the glow of the setting sun.

Pepsi whistled for Lightning to hunt. In the gathering dusk, the birds of the Chesapeake were active. Pepsi prayed that Lightning's hunt would be a fast one.

Then high in the air, everyone saw the great falcon plummet. Like an arrow she hurled down and struck her target. In an instant she returned, drifting gracefully down into the Algonquin village. In her talons she carried a plump duck. She dropped it right at Pepsi's feet, and the crowd gasped again. Pepsi picked up the game bird and presented it to the stunned old Quiyow. Then he lifted his arm in signal, and his perfectly trained falcon landed in her place.

Then villagers around him fell back, and gazed at Pepsicanough and his hunting bird with wide-eyed awe and wonder. There was nothing more the old Quiyow could say. He turned and walked away.

"The Huskanaw is over!" proclaimed Opech.

The drums started to play again, first quietly and then with more passion. This time the sound was joyous and full of celebration. The men and women, dressed in their finest buckskins, began to move gracefully around the circle, and the dancing began. Pepsi sat at the edge of the circle and observed the beautiful procession. He marvelled at their rhythmic dance moves. Soon the story dancers began. Pepsi listened closely to the words of the chants that told about generations of young boys growing to manhood. There were dances about deer hunting, dances about wolves and mountain lions, and of course, a dance that told the story of a great bear.

The celebration continued into the night. They sang about the history of The People. About how, long ago, they traveled from a land in the west. They sang of great battles, and even about his own grandfather, the great Powhatan. Hours passed, and yet the people continued to dance and sing. Sometimes Pepsi joined in the dancing. Sometimes he just sat and watched, and learned.

Midway through the night, Pepsi's eyes searched the crowd for Parahunt. He had not seen him for hours. Where was his uncle, his teacher? He had expected him to stay by his side and celebrate this great moment. Pepsi wanted to share this victory with his uncle. He knew that without Parahunt's wisdom and teaching he never could have survived the Huskanaw.

And as Parahunt had said, *The God of Pocahontas went with him.*

It was during those excruciating days of fasting and prayer that Pepsi began to understand his need to break the endless circle of revenge and hate—it was time to forgive Uncle Opech. And at that moment, he chose to do whatever it would take to gain his position on the Council of the Chiefs of the Algonquin. Because only by this power, could he become a force of peace between English and Algonquin.

In the early hours of morning, the drumming died down and finally stopped. The honored men and women stood around the circle looking toward him. A silence washed over the tribe as Opech raised both arms and made the official proclamation.

"This day, we present Chief Pepsicanough. He has the blood-rite of Powhatan and of Pocahontas. He has completed the Huskanaw. He is now a chief of the Algonquin. We receive Chief Pepsicanough with honor."

Just then, at the edge of the circle, Pepsicanough noticed that Parahunt had joined the crowd. And by the bonfire's light, he could see that Parahunt had someone with him. The small figure was that of an English woman. She stepped forward into closer view—it was his Jane! He stood straight and tall, receiving the honor and congratulations of the tribe, but in his heart he longed to run to Jane and throw his arms around her. He knew that would not be fitting behavior for an Algonquin Chief. But his eyes met hers across the flickering firelight and he knew she understood.

The sky began to glow with the first sign of morning, and the tired crowd began to trickle off to their wigwams. Pepsi slowly made his way over to Parahunt and Jane. It seemed like a lifetime since he had left her back at Varina to tend to Kevin.

"Pepsi!" she exclaimed. "I made Parahunt promise to return to me as soon as you finished your testing. And when he told me the good news, I *had* to come! I *had* to congratulate you!" She looked down shyly. "I hope you don't mind."

"Of course not! I was so happy to see you." He turned to Parahunt. "Thank you for bringing her." His voice choked a little as he continued. "And thank you, Uncle, for everything. I could not have made it without your help."

"You will be a good chief, Pepsicanough." Parahunt's face shone with pride. "I am certain that as you sit on the Council, you will lead the Powhatans to a treaty of peace. Now it is time to go home."

The three of them walked down to Parahunt's canoe. He would take them back to Varina. Pepsi walked between his uncle and the woman he still hoped to marry—his two favorite people! And suddenly he realized that he, Thomas Pepsicanough Rolfe, would spend the rest of his days between Parahunt and Jane—between Algonquin and English—between *Two Mighty Rivers*.

*   *   *

AFTERWORD

History has given us many facts about Thomas Pepsicanough Rolfe. As a young child, he sailed with his parents to England, where John Rolfe and Pocahontas became famous for their adventures. In 1617, just as they were sailing back to the New World, Pocahontas became ill and died. But her dying wish was that her son would be "raised with a good education in the ways of God."

To honor this request, John Rolfe placed young Thomas in the care of his family, while he returned to Virginia. Thomas was raised in Norfolk and educated at Cambridge.

But as he was learning and seeking his faith, much turmoil was uprooting both England and the New World. England was rocked by religious persecution and political unrest, which eventually led to a civil war. And in the New World, hatred between the natives and the settlers led to bloodshed. Opech became the leader of the Algonquins after Powhatan's death. When an English settler killed an Algonquin warrior, Opech took his revenge in an event that became known as the Massacre of 1622.

We know that Thomas Pepsicanough Rolfe was said to be unusually tall and strong, with the attractive features and courageous spirit of his mother. There are records of John Rolfe's letters, which influenced his son's faith; and a communication from Opech to the Virginia Company which invited Pepsi to claim his inheritance among the Algonquins.

After Pepsi confronted Opech and went through the Huskanaw, he joined the Algonquin Council of Chiefs, and the

English and Opech signed a new peace treaty. Thomas Pepsi-canough Rolfe married his sweetheart, Jane Poythress, and took her to live happily on his farm, Varina. Pepsi and Jane had one little girl, whom they named Jane Rebecca. Pepsi died in the Chesapeake at the age of eighty-seven.

BIBLIOGRAPHY

Manuscript Materials

Letter from John Rolfe to Sir Thomas Dale, MS Ashmoleam 830, folder 118-19.

Letter from John Rolfe to Sir Edwin Sandys, June 8, 1617. Box IX, Doc. 961, Cambridge University. Magdalene College.

A True Relation of the State of Virginia, by Mr. J. Rolfe. May 9, 1619. Box 1, Doc. 208. Duke of Manchester Papers, updated by the University of Virginia Press.

Early Records of Virginia. Safe 13, 2 Vols., 1607-1622, Library of Congress Publications Services, Washington, D.C.

Grant to John Smith, 1619. Grant Book, Public Records Office of London, Vol. LXXXIX, MS 217.

Printed Pamphlets

The Generall Historie of Virginie, New England and the Summer Isles. Printed in London by J. Dawson and J. Haviland for Michael Sparks, 1624.

Index to Writings on American History, Washington D.C., U.S. Government Printing Office, 1956.

New World: the First Pictures of America as Done by John White and Jacques Le Moyne. New York, Duell, Sloane and Pierce, 1946.

Good Newes From Virginia by the Rev. Alexander Whitaker. Scholars Facsimiles and Reprints of New York. (Originally printed in London, 1616.)

Books and Articles

Aiken, Lucy. *The Court of King James I*, 2 Vols. London: 1822.

Barbour, Phillip L. *The Three Worlds of Captain John Smith*. Boston: Houghton Mifflin Company, 1964.

Brown, Alexander. *The Genesis of the United States*. Boston: Houghton Mifflin Company, 1890.

Churchill, Winston. *The New World* (1485–1688). Vol II in *A History of the English Speaking Peoples*. New York: Dodd, Mead and Company, 1956.

Davids, J. *The First Settlers of Virginia*. New York: Riley and Company, 1806.

Dickens, Charles. *A Child's History of England*. New York: G.W. Carlton and Company, 1878.

Feest, Christian F. *The Powhatan Tribes*. New York: Chelsea House Publishers, 1979.

Gruden, Robert Pierce. *A History of Gravesend*. London: William Pickering and Company. For James Johnston. 1848.

Lewis, Clifford M. and Albert Loomis. *The Spanish Mission in Virginia, 1570–1572*. Chapel Hill: University of North Carolina Press, 1953.

Mooney, James. "The Powhatan Confederacy, Past and Present." *American Anthropology*. Vol 9, No. 1 (January 1907): 123–29.

Purchas, Samuel. *Purchas, His Pilgrimes*. Glasgow: James MacLehose and Sons, 1904. (First printed in 1630.)

Robertson, Wyndham. *Pocahontas and her Descendants*. Richmond, Va.: J.W. Randolf, 1887.

Roundtree, Helen C. *The Powhatan Indians of Virginia Through Four Centuries*. Norman, Okla.: University of Oklahoma Press, 1990.

Smith, Captain John. *Travels and Workes of Captain John Smith In His Own Words.* Ed. by Edward Arber and A.G. Bradley, 2 Vols. Edinburgh: John Grants Publishers, 1910.

Wilson, George F. *Saints and Strangers.* New York: Reynal and Hitchcock, 1945.

Winsor, John Dover, Ed. *Life in Shakespeare's England.* Baltimore: Penguin Books, Inc., 1959.

Woodward, Grace Steele. *Pocahontas.* Norman, Okla.: University of Oklahoma Press, 1969.

Interview with Mrs. Mayflower Adkins, tribal leader, Chickahominy Tribe. Charles City, Va. 1996.